Leadership Review Handbook

by

Dr. Anis I. Milad, D.B.A., S.C.P.M.

authorHOUSE®

AuthorHouse™
1663 Liberty Drive
Bloomington, IN 47403
www.authorhouse.com
Phone: 1-800-839-8640

First published by AuthorHouse   4/26/2010

ISBN: 978-1-4520-0968-1 (e)
ISBN: 978-1-4520-0967-4 (sc)

Library of Congress Control Number: 2010905515

Printed in the United States of America
Bloomington, Indiana

This book is printed on acid-free paper.

Contents

CEOs and the Board of Directors

CEOs and the Board of Directors

Introduction

CEOs-board of directors' relationship is based on trust. The job of the board of directors is to monitor and discipline the CEO. The executives are considered rivals who are contesting and criticizing the decisions of the CEO. The informal power of the CEO increases her/his chances of controlling regardless of performance. The inside board of directors are not the best for the job because they are beholden their positions and careers to the CEO. The board follows rules and these are formal rules of corporate governance which depend on committees of outside directors for setting executive reimbursement, monitoring corporate audits, all capital expenditure decisions over a certain amount, standardization of the CEO succession, and selection procedure.

Literature Review

The relationship between the CEO and the board of directors depends on many elements. The informal power of the CEO plays a role in the life of the organization. While, informal CEO power or firm performance is elevated, the threat of CEO defenses is also elevated, creating more dysfunctional duality. While informal CEO power or firm performance is near to the ground, CEO defenses is less expected to take place, and there is strain for strong leadership, creating more non-duality dysfunctional (Finkelstein & Aveni, 1994). On the other hand, executive teams are, above all, imperative determinants of organizational results in that they are at the edge between an organization and its environment. Executive teams intervene between external environmental demands and internal organizational dynamics (Keck & Tushman, 1993). In contrast, agency theorists recognize that boards will be different in their motivation to monitor for the benefit of shareholders; as a product, motivations are a main originator to successful monitoring (Lynall, Golden & Hillman, 2003).

Although, many new CEOs do not have the experience, resources, or reputations of their predecessors, they extend decision-making ability more broadly because they have to depend on other administrators for both political support and information (Miller, 1993). Rules form and are created by political procedures, they are not only the likeness of decision makers but are created by history and experience and are not easily changed in response to the immediate interests of organizational decision makers (Ocasio, 1999). It is important to note that the CEO succession has a small effect on performance (Ocasio, 1994). In Contrast, another research pointed out that relationships between board structure and organizational outcomes are affected significantly by interpersonal influence processes in CEO-board relationships (Westphal, 1998). Many studies suggested that leading point of view on CEO-board relationships essentially suggests that structural board independence adds to the board power in particular in its relationship with the CEO. Many studies have simply connected structural independence with board power while others have argued how CEOs take advantage of structural bases of power to maintain ultimate control over the board (Westphal, 1998).

Today, there are a fewer bodies of research on CEO duality. In a current study CEO duality was negatively associated with the organization performance. In contrast, many other studies have found performance and duality to be not related (Finkelstein & D Aveni, 1994). Changes in environmental setting or changes in a firm's strategic orientation, or both may be driving forces in that they create new capability requirements for executive teams (Keck & Tushman, 1993). A model suggests a four stage life cycle comprising the forming of the board of directors: 1) an entrepreneurial stage (early innovation, niche formation, creativity), 2) a collectivity stage (high cohesion, commitment), 3) a formalization and control stage (stability and institutionalization), and 4) an elaboration of structure stage (domain expansion and decentralization) (Lynall, Golden & Hillman, 2003).

However, the new CEO must be aware of constructing agreements behind their suggestion. Hence, compared to their precursors, apprentice CEOs will hand over more authority for both routine and strategic decisions (Miller, 1993). The board follows rules and these are formal rules of corporate governance which depends on committees of outside directors for setting executive reimbursement, monitoring corporate audits, all capital expenditure decisions over a certain amount, standardization of the CEO succession, and selection procedure. However, informal rules of corporate governance includes restrictions on open criticism of the CEO, not contacting fellow board members outside of meetings, and, for most boards, using the language of shareholder interests to clarify board decisions (Ocasio, 1999).

Ironically, according to the model of circulation, the CEO's increasing by outdated style triggers opportunities for contesting his power. Executive officers of the corporations are challengers for the CEO's power and position (Ocasio, 1994). On the other hand, the board independence may force the CEO to use interpersonal power tactics that drastically counteract the effect of structural independence on the board's overall power to defend shareholders (Westphal, 1998) In contrast, "increases in structural board independence lead to larger subsequent increases in CEO compensation by increasing the level of CEO interpersonal influence behavior" (Westphal, 1998).

A monitoring board leans toward a large group of independent, outside directors--individuals not otherwise inside directors who are affiliated with the firm on whose board they sit. The outside directors are more alert than inside directors because "(1) they focus on financial performance, which is a central component of monitoring; (2) they are more likely than insiders to dismiss CEOs following poor performance" (Finkelstein & Aveni, 1994).

While the long period of incremental changes able the board to form some facts suggests that organizations grow through relatively long periods of incremental changes in service to a precise strategic orientation, emphasized by reorientations (Keck & Tushman, 1993). However, a board can be formed at several stages of the firm's growth (Lynall, Golden & Hillman, 2003). In contrast, most new CEOs know they are not as knowledgeable as the previous CEOs with the performance and problems of their organizations. Nor are they usually as familiar about the collection of functions and departments; as a result, they settle for less (Miller, 1993).

On the other hand, the succession of an insider versus an outsider as CEO offers an essential environment for maintaining an institutionalized action standpoint on corporate control. The CEO succession process naturally is vision as an instrument for organizational adaptation. It is guided by the formal and informal rules of corporate governance. Outsider succession, especially, has been known as a trigger of organizational change (Ocasio, 1999). In contrast, CEOs with more broad board seniority become out-of-date because they are more likely to maintain the policies and programs of the corporation instituted while they were members of the board and may be less open to organizational change (Ocasio, 1994).

The segment of the board composed of outside directors represents one perspective of formal structural independence from management. "While both inside and outside directors are responsible for overseeing corporate strategy, agency theory and legal perspectives on corporate boards emphasize that outsiders have the potential to evaluate strategic decision making more objectively" (Westphal, 1998).

The differences between the vigilant board and non-vigilant board are significant. For example, non-vigilant boards do not have the power to scrutinize and punish CEOs because they are mostly inside directors, and insiders may be indebted to a CEO for their livelihood (Finkelstein & Aveni, 1994). Also, "Vigilant boards tend to favor non-duality because duality, by providing CEOs with undivided formal authority, promotes CEO entrenchment and, hence, can lead to opportunistic and inefficient behavior that reduces shareholder wealth" (Finkelstein & Aveni, 1994). In addition, the challenge for control within the board of directors is not one of predetermined loyalties, of insiders seeking protection versus outsiders monitoring performance, but one of evolving power struggles, conditioned on environmental contingencies and economic returns. Both insiders and outsiders combining power are to be merging into single entity (Ocasio, 1994).

Although, the board of directors will end as one unit they might be ill equipped to influence the organization's performance at a later stage of the organization (Lynall, Golden & Hillman, 2003). Previous studies have also suggested that interpersonal processes influence the CEO and among the board members can provide another source of power to structural position, such that individuals can use ingratiation and persuasion tactics to enhance their overall power despite whether or not they hold significant structural sources of power in the organization (Westphal, 1998). In contrast, The interpersonal process is not the only factor to successful leadership but the past experiences of CEOs may minimize or reverse the inability effects which are related to CEO tenure (Keck & Tushman, 1993).

Conclusion

CEO duality is crucial to the organization. The CEO is able to control both the executives and the board of directors. CEO's duality decreases the shareholders' chance to earn their rights. The informal CEO power increases her/his control on the organization, perhaps, to dismiss the rights of the shareholders for personal goals. The outside board of directors is suitable for the development of the organization. The outside board members will be concerned for the wealth of stockholders and the compensation and discipline of the CEO.

References

Finkelstien, S. D & Aveni, R. (994). CEO duality as a double-edged sword: How boards of directors balance entrenchment avoidance and unity of command. <u>Academy of</u> <u>Management Journal.</u> Briarcliff Manor: Vol. 37, Iss. 5; pg. 1079, 30 pgs. Retrieved February 18, 2004 from ProQuest website: http://www.umi.com/proquest/

Keck, S. & Tushman, M. (1993). Environmental and organizational context and executive team. <u>Academy of Management Journal</u>. Briarcliff Manor: Vol. 36, Iss. 6; pg 1314, 31 pgs. Retrieved February 18, 2004 from ProQuest website: http://www.umi.com/proquest/

Lynall, M., Golden, B.,& Hillman, A. (2003). Board composition from adolescence to maturity: A multitheoretic view. <u>Academy of Management Review</u>, 03637425, Vol. 28, Issue 3. Retrieved February 18, 2004 from EBSCOHost website: http://ejournals. ebsco.com/login.asp?bCookiesEnabled=TRUE

Miller, D. (1993). Some organizational consequences of CEO succession. Academy of Management Journal. Briarcliff Manor: Vo. 36, Iss. 3; pg 644, 16 pgs. Retrieved February 18, 2004 from ProQuest website: http://www.umi.com/proquest/

Ocasio, W. (1994). Political dynamics and the circulation of power: CEO succession in U.S. industrial corporations, 1960-1990. Administrative Science Quarterly. Ithaca: Vol. 39, Iss. 2; pg.285, 28 pgs. Retrieved February 18, 2004 from ProQuest website: http://www.umi.com/proquest/

Ocasio, W. (1999). Institutionalized action and corporate governance: The reliance on rules of CEO succession. Administrative Science Quarterly. Ithaca: Vol. 44, Iss. 2; pg 384, 33 pgs. Retrieved February 18, 2004 from ProQuest website: http://www.umi.com/proquest/

Westphal, J. (1998). Board games: How CEOs adapt to increases in structural board independence from management. Administrative Science Quarterly. Ithaca: Vol. 43, Iss. 3; pg. 511, 27 pgs. Retrieved February 18, 2004 from ProQuest website: http://www.umi.com/proquest/

Leadership and Culture

Leadership and Culture

Literature Review

There are many empirical articles about organizational culture and leadership. Scholars agree that the culture is about implementation and carrying out the characteristics of the organization. The researchers shift "the focus from strategy formulation to strategy execution—and culture is all about execution" (Chatman & Cha, 2003). Culture plays a role in the life of the organization and employees because "The irony of leadership through culture is that the less formal direction you give employees about how to execute strategy, the more ownership they take over their actions and the better they perform" (Chatman & Cha, 2003).

The Culture of the Founder

Employees communicate and are empowered by the culture of the founder or the leader "Unlike formal rules, policies, and procedures, culture empowers employees to think and act on their own in pursuit of strategic objectives, increasing their commitment to those goals" (Chatman & Cha, 2003). Although, the concept sounds scholarly the phenomena of the classroom make this concept less convincing. Schein states that "If we are teachers, we encounter the sometimes mysterious phenomenon that different classes behave completely differently from each other even though our material and teaching style remain the same" (Schein, 1997, p. 4). So the culture might not be the direct result of the leader as stated in the following statement, "Organizational cultures are often the creation of their entrepreneurial founders. Founders often create an organizational culture from a preconceived 'cultural scheme' in their head. Typically, the founder's and his or her successor's leadership helps shape a culture of shared values and assumptions guided and restricted by the founders' personal beliefs. The success or failure of an organization depends on the relevance of the founder's philosophical beliefs to the current opportunities and constraints (which are) confronting the organization" (Bass & Avolio, 1993).

It is understandable that "The concept of culture helps explain all of these phenomena and to 'normalize' them" (Schein, 1997, p. 4), but if "different classes behave differently" then the culture has a little to do with the leader or the founder. Employees probably have their own culture which they bring to the place of work, in contrast, "members of professional cultures, however, consider their private lives to be their own business. They feel that the organization hires on the basis of job competence only, and they do think far ahead" (Hofstede, 1998).

The Organizational Culture

The organization is a complex structure. The incentive and control are important parts of the success of an organization, "Leaders and executives think in terms of such systems of incentives and controls and are concerned about shared values and beliefs because they are dealing with thousands rather than a few immediate subordinates, and it is their ability to organize thousands that creates some of the most effective organizations we have seen" (Schein, 1996). Organization behavior is well documented. The shared values contribute to the success of the organization.

In Hofstede's empirical research argues that the culture of the employees depends on the perception of the employees, "Dimension 2 explores the differences between a concern for people and a concern for getting the job done. The key items selected show that, in the employee-oriented cultures, people feel that their personal problems are taken into account, that the organization takes a responsibility for employee welfare, and that important decisions tend to be made by groups or committees. In the job-oriented units, people experience a strong pressure for getting the job done. They perceive the organization as only being interested in the work employees do, not in their personal and family welfare; and they report that important decisions tend to be made by individuals" (Hofstede, 1998). In contrast, the culture in other scholars' findings is forced when the organization is young "Though strong organizational cultures have long been touted as critical to bottom-line performance in large organizations,19 newer evidence from a unique sample suggests that developing a strong, strategically relevant culture may be best accomplished when an organization is young" (Chatman & Cha, 2003).

Culture according to the literature can mold the newcomers to support their cultures and their cultures need to be adapted to the new thinking, "Most creativity research has focused on hiring creative people, but innovation may depend more on whether cultural norms support risk-taking and change" (Chatman & Cha, 2003). In contrast, there are speculations that cultures blend and emerge. For example, thinking the globalization exists among the nations is not very accurate according to Hofstede who states that "There are no globally universal business goals. Globalization is often more a slogan and wishful thinking than a reality" (Hofstede et al, 2002). Prior to merging different cultures "We need to understand better what the forces are that cause organizations of all kinds to create similar cultural milieu (setting), incentive and control systems that operate in the same way, even though the goals of the organizations are quite different" (Schein, 1996). Ironically, scholars are swinging between the impossible merger among cultures in the concept of the global village and the possibility of the merger of cultures, "I assumed that the unique history of an organization would eventually override the prior cultural assumptions of all of their employees" (Schein, 1996).

Creating Shared Beliefs

Leaders are important to direct the followers and changing their beliefs for the good of the organization. Scholars argue that "Leaders also promote innovation by creating a shared beliefs that team members are safe to take interpersonal risks" (Chatman & Cha, 2003). Creating shared beliefs might not be a change for the best of the team. Creating shared belief must be learned by each individual, "Learning is, however, a basically individualistic concept drawn directly from psychology, where it is highly developed, and we have not yet settled on a good definition of what it might mean for an organization to learn" (Schein, 1996). If the leader changes the beliefs of the followers the change will be associated directly from psychology of the followers. However, the leaders should care and "need to be attentive to the conservativeness reflected in beliefs, values, assumptions, rites, and ceremonies embedded in the culture that can hinder efforts to change the organization. They need to modify key aspects of culture, when it is possible to do so, to fit with new directions desired by the leadership and membership of the organization" (Bass & Avolio, 1993)

The Culture and the Assumptions

The culture of the organization affects the leader as well as the subordinates, "The organization's culture develops in large part from its leadership while the culture of an organization can also affect the development of its leadership" (Bass & Avolio, 1993). On the other hand, organization cannot survive and succeed only on the organization's culture but surviving requires strategic thinking, "Effective organizations require both tactical and strategic thinking as well as culture building by its leaders. To reiterate, the culture affects leadership as much as leadership affects culture" (Bass & Avolio, 1993). But the culture and the assumptions of the employees in an organization is important to understand change and success as Schein argues that "We are in grave danger of not seeing our own culture, our assumptions about methods, about theory, about what is important to study or not study, and, in that process, pay too much attention only to what suits our needs" (Schein, 1996). It is the culture that improves creativity and the improvement of productivity because "Leaders who are concerned about organizational renewal will seek to foster organizational cultures that are hospitable and conducive to creativity, problem solving, risk taking, and experimentation" (Bass & Avolio, 1993)

Assumptions are strong as reality. Actually our assumptions make our reality. If our assumptions put to the test we will be under attack and develop anxiety; however, "The human mind needs cognitive stability. Therefore, any challenge to or questioning of a basic assumption will release anxiety and defensiveness. (Schein, 1997, p. 23). Therefore, leaders are obligated to understand the depth of the role of the culture in organizations, or group because "The most central issue for leaders, therefore, is how to get at the deeper levels of a culture, how to assess the functionality of the assumption made at each level, and how to deal with ate anxiety that is unleashed when those levels are challenged. (Schein, 1997, p. 27).

Probably, it seems That the founders or the leaders' "primary role (is) to develop and maintain an effective culture" (Chatman & Cha, 2003). There are skeptical scholars who are not sure that practices are designed according to the value of the founders or the leaders. Hofstede (1998) argues that "we believe that an organization's culture is located in the mental programmes of all members of the organization. There is little doubt that practices are designed according to the values of the founders and, in later phases, of significant top managers of the organization in question, but this does not mean that all members of the organization share these values" (Hofstede, 1998).

Reference

Bass, B. & Avolio, B. (1993). Transformational leadership and organizational culture. Public Administration Quarterly. Vol. 17, Iss. 1; pg. 112, 10 pgs. Retrieved January 22, 2004 from Pro Quest website: http://www.umi.com/proquest/

Chatman, J. & Cha, S. (2003) Leading by leveraging culture. California Management Review. Vol. 45, No 4. Retrieved January 22, 2004 from Pro Quest website: http://www.umi.com/proquest/

Hofstede, G. (1998). Attitudes, values and organizational culture: Disentangling the concepts. Organization Studies. Vol. 19, Iss. 3; pg. 477, 17 pgs. Retrieved January 22, 2004 from Pro Quest website: http://www.umi.com/proquest/

Hofstede, G. (1980). Culture consequences: International differences in work-related values. New bury Park: SAGE Publication

Hofstede, G. et al. (2002). What goals do business leaders pursue? A study in fifteen countries. Journal of International Business Studies. 33,4 (Fourth Quarter): 785-803. Retrieved January 22, 2004 from Pro Quest website: http://www.umi.com/proquest/

Schein, E. (1996). Culture: The missing concept in organization studies. Administrative Science Quarterly. Vol. 41, Iss. 2; pg. 229, 12 pgs. Retrieved January 22, 2004 from Pro Quest website: http://www. umi.com/proquest/

Schein, E. (1997) Organizational culture and leadership. San Francisco: Jossy-Bass

Outline for Case Study:
Barnard and Selznick

Outline for Case Study:
Barnard and Selznick

Introduction

Warren Bennis in his book entitled *On Becoming a Leader* said that "Learning to lead is, on one level, learning to manage change" (Bennis, 1989, Page 145). The problem which is created by Chester Barnard and Philip Selznick are the ambiguous ideas and philosophies of the role of leadership which both presented in their books. Leadership, however, as described by Barnard, is not learning to manage change but a moral element (Barnard, 1938, Page 259). On the other hand, Selznick's definition of leadership and leaders is that the leader is an agent of institutionalization offering a guiding hand to a process that would otherwise occur more haphazardly, more readily subject to the accident of circumstances and history" (Selznick, 1957, Page 27).

Thesis

Leaders, who acquire leadership skills, are able to change the status quo at any level in the organization, initiate proposals and guide subordinates to perform their tasks throughout the change, during the "unfreeze" of the old systems and technology, during the implementation of change, and during the institutionalization.

Arguments

Argument 1: Leadership is not only done by people in authority, high prestige, or decision makers.

Argument 2: Leadership is learned and experienced in contrast with the idea which claims that leaders are born.

Argument 3: Leadership is the kind of work done to meet a change in organization and a social situation.

The similarities between Barnard and Selznick:

1) Both authors include in their books the psychological and social factors in the system and the basic psychophysical aspects of behavior.

2) Both authors defined the purpose and commitment of the organization.

3) Both authors also agreed that communication and commitment are important organizational structures.

4) "Barnard (1938) text, The Functions of the Executive, is a substantial primer on leadership that resonates a profoundly humanistic ethic" (Aupperle & Dunphy, 2001). Steven P. Feldman considers the unethical behavior a result of depersonalized relationship in which it destroys the dedication of the person (Feldman, 1996). On the other hand, Selznick promotes social values which "are objects of desire that are of sustaining group identity" (Sezenick, 1956, 121).

The differences between Barnard and Selznick:

1) Barnard focuses on the executive level but Selznick focuses on the social aspects of all levels of the organization.

2) Barnard defines the formal and informal organization but Selznick defines the organization and institution.

3) Barnard "refers to society as a complex of informal organizations" and his discussion of cultural context is vague and misleading (Feldman, 1996). On the other hand, Slezinck is clear in his definition of the society, that is, "there will be quick assent to the proposition that a democratic constitution is strong or weak according to the culture and social organization upon which it rests. A strong constitutional system is built into the underlying social structure." (Selznick, 1956, 91). It seems that Barnard

doesn't have clear understanding of the social structure as much as Selznick.

Conclusion

Barnard's and Selznick's researches were not based on 1) Experimental research, 2) Ethnography, 3) Case study, or 4) Survey, but both writers based their researches on theories, observation, and opinion. The researches of both authors lean toward qualitative research. Both authors left the door ajar for further research in this important field of leadership.

References

Aupperle, K. & Dunphy, S. (2001). *Managerial Lessons for New Millennium: Contributions from Chester Barnard and Frank Capra.* Management Decision. Vol 39 No 2 2001 pp 156-164. MCB University Press ISSN 0025-1747. Retrieved December 15, 2003 from Emerald Database Website: http://giorgio.emeraldinsight.com/vl=25934534/cl=13/nw=1/rpsv/cgi-bin/emft.pl Barnard, C. (1938). *The Functions of the Executive.* Massachusetts: Harvard University Press.

Bennis, W. (1989). *On Becoming a Leader.* New York: Addison-Wesley Publishing Company.

Feldman, S. (1996) The disinheritance of Management Ethics: Rational Individualism in Barnard's The Function of the Executive. Journal of Management History. Vol. 2 No. 4 1996. pp 34-47. MCB University Press ISSN 1355-252X. Retrieved December 15, 2003 from Emerald Database Website: http://giorgio.emeraldinsight. com/vl=25934534/cl=13/nw=1/rpsv/cgi-bin/emft.pl

Feldman, S. (1996). *Incorporating the Contrary: The Politics of Dichotomy in Chester Barnard's Organization Sociology.* Journal of Management History. Vol. 2 No. 2 1996 pp 26-40. MCB University Press ISSN 1355-252X. Retrieved December 15, 2003 from Emerald Database Website: http://giorgio.emeraldinsight.com/vl=25934534/cl=13/ nw=1/rpsv/cgi-bin/emft.pl

Selznick, P. (1956). *Leadership in Administration a Sociological Interpretation.* California: University of California Press.

Path-Goal theory of Leadership

Path-Goal theory of Leadership: Outline

I. Thesis: The Path-Goal theory of leadership is a classic theory of leadership with limitation, but the transformational leadership and the charismatic leadership are both concerned, in depth, about the followers and the followers-leader relationship; however, the charismatic leadership is precarious if the leader exercises its dark side.

II. Introduction: The transformational leadership is based on the leaders' understanding to the followers. S/he is supportive and empowers the subordinates to be creative. The path-goal theory reflects the relationship between the involvement of the leader and the followers. On the other hand, the charismatic leadership is based on the leader personal charisma and the perception of the followers. The charismatic leader could become destructive of others.

III. The Transformational Leadership and Path-Goal Classic Leadership

1) Transforming Leadership and The Leaders' end Value

2) Path-Goal theory and The Charismatic Leader

IV. The contrast Between Transformational Leadership and the Charismatic Leadership

1) The Goal of the Transforming Leader

2) Understanding the relationships between the Charismatic Leader and the followers

V. Charismatic Leader between Right and Wrong

1) Personal Characteristics and the Clear Vision

2) The Charismatic Leader and the Dark side

3) The Limitation of the Charismatic Leader

VI. The Leader as a Change Agent

1) Transformational Change and Employee Morale

2) Charismatic Leader as a Change Agent

VII. Conclusion: The transformational leader works with the subordinates closely to achieve the goal of the organization. The path-goal theory reflects the relationship between the involvement of the leader and the followers. The relationships between charismatic leader and the followers are based on the perception and attribution the followers make. The dark side of the charismatic leadership occurs when the leader takes advantage of the followers' perception of her/his image.

Path-Goal theory of Leadership

I. Thesis:

The Path-Goal theory of leadership is a classic theory of leadership with limitation, but the transformational leadership and the charismatic leadership are both concerned, in depth, about the followers and the followers-leader relationship; however, the charismatic leadership is precarious if the leader exercises its dark side..

II. Introduction:

The transformational leadership is based on the leaders' understanding of the followers. S/he is supportive and empowers the subordinates to be creative. S/he is working with the subordinates closely to achieve the goal of the organization. The subordinates share the vision of the leader and they blend their personal goals with the goals of the organization. The path-goal theory reflects the relationship between the involvement of the leader and the followers. On the other hand, the charismatic leadership is based on the leader's personal charisma and of the perception of her/him by the followers. The charismatic leader creates her/his image as an extraordinary leader. The dark side of the charismatic leadership occurs when the leader takes advantage of the followers' perception of her/his image. The dark side of the charismatic leader is that s/he could become destructive of others.

III. The Transformational Leadership and Path-Goal Classic Leadership

1. Transforming Leadership and the Leaders' end Value

The transformational leadership is concerned about the relationship between the leader and the followers and to encourage them to reach their maximum potential, "Transformational leaders motivate followers to accept and accomplish difficult goals that followers normally would not have pursued" (Kuhnert & Lewis, 1987). The leader is working very hard to convince the followers to adopt her/his vision because transformational leadership effects organizational change through the articulation of leaders' vision, the acceptance of the vision by followers, and the creation of a congruence between followers' self-interests and the vision" (Pawar & Eastman, 1997).

2. Path-Goal theory and The Charismatic Leader

The Path-Goal theory of leadership claims that "The lower the task structure (routinization, standardization, etc.) of subordinates, (1) the higher the relationship and role clarity, and (2) the lower the relationship between supportive leader behavior and the same dependent variable" (Schriesheim, 1977). The path-goal theory reflects the relationship between the involvement of the leader and the followers. On the other hand, the "charismatic value based leadership is also required, or is at least more effective, in situations that require a combination of highly involved and active leadership plus emotional commitment and extraordinary effort by both leaders and followers" (House, 1996)

IV. The contrast Between Transformational Leadership and the Charismatic Leadership

1. The Goal of the Transforming Leader

Followers of the transforming leader are concerned about the task and to achieve the goal of the organization, "followers of transformational leaders viewed their work as more important and as more self-congruent" (Bono & Judge, 2003). The goal of the leader becomes the goal of the subordinates because the leader empowers and supports them, "transforming leader makes contact with employees at all levels ..... Gives attention and recognition to others' strength .... And speaks about a future vision, goal, and plan" (Anderson, 1992, p 51). The Sheldon and Elliot define self-concordance as extension to transformational leadership as follows, "Self-concordance refers to the extent to which activities such as job-related tasks or goals express individuals' authentic interest and value" (Bono & Judge, 2003). Therefore, the characteristic of the relationship between transforming leadership and self-concordance is dissimilar. "In the field study, transformational leadership was positively correlated with autonomous motivation but not with controlled motivation. The opposite was true in the experiment, where transformational leadership had its strongest effect on controlled motivation" (Bono & Judge, 2003).

2. Understanding the relationships between the Charismatic Leader and the followers

"Transformational and charismatic theories have been framed to recognize the affective and emotional needs and responses of followers" (Bono & Judge, 2003). Actually, the relationships between charismatic leader and the followers are based on the perception and attribution the followers make. Not only the perception makes the followers obey the leader but "charismatic leaders transform the nature of work (in this case, work meant to achieve the organization's vision) by making it appear more heroic, morally correct, and meaningful" (Conger, 1999). The myth and the creative stories and the distance of the charismatic leader contribute to the fictional relationship between the charismatic leader and her/his followers; "Yet the majority of the literature in the field sees vision as a component of charismatic leadership. Furthermore, Max Weber believed that the basis for charismatic leadership was a perception by followers that their leader was extraordinary" (Conger, 1999).

V. Charismatic Leader between Right and Wrong

1. Personal Characteristics and the Clear Vision

It is important for the charismatic leader to have personal characteristic and vision. Weber defines charisma when he said "Charisma, meaning literally 'gift of grace' is used by Weber to characterize self-appointed leaders who are followed by those who are in distress and who need to follow the leader because they believe him to be extraordinarily qualified" (Weber, 1946, p52). On the other hand, Waldman & Yammarino, (1999) went further in their definition of the charismatic leader; they said that "we define CEO charisma in two parts. First, it is based on behavioral tendencies and personal characteristics of the leader, including the articulation of a clear vision derived from firmly held values or moral justifications, role modeling of those values, communication of high performance expectations and confidence in followers' abilities to meet those expectations, references to the greater collective and its identity, symbolic behaviors, and the assumption of personal risks and sacrifices" (Waldman & Yammarino, 1999). In addition, "the greater the discrepancy of the vision from the status quo, the more likely is the attribution that the leader has extraordinary vision, not just an ordinary goal." (Conger, 1999)

2. The Charismatic Leader and the Dark side

In history, we have learned that the followers obey the leader if s/he has the image that makes her/him an extraordinary. The perception the followers make for the charismatic leader is critical for the leader. Sometimes people create stories about the leader and how intelligent the leader is and intend to "use of organizational stories, rites and rituals, symbols, slogans, logos, and other cultural elements, the CEO can provide those at a distance with a picture of the organization" (Waldman & Yammarino, 1999). The charismatic leader, unlike the transforming leader, is capable of abusing her/his power, "it is possible for a charismatic leader to be more personalized or immoral, that is, self-serving or exploitative of others (Waldman & Yammarino, 1999). The charismatic leader prefers to create a bubble around her/him and to keep an illusionary status; however, the charismatic leader has to keep her/his distance between her/himself and the followers because the charismatic leaders realize "the importance of considering the social distance between leaders and followers" (Waldman & Yammarino, 1999).

3. The Limitation of the Charismatic Leader

It is not very often to see that the western world goes under a bad charismatic leader but when it happens the world will be on the edge of wars. The "organizational cultures may prevent charismatic leaders from emerging or being chosen externally, even though the environmental circumstances may necessitate such leadership" (Waldman & Yammarino, 1999). If the people are aware and have the power to vote on the level of the group, organization, or nation the dark side of the charismatic leadership will fade before it happens.

VI. Charismatic Leader as a Change Agent

Conger emphasizes that charismatic leaders are always seen as organizational reformers or entrepreneurs. In other words, "they act as agents of innovative and radical change" (Conger, 1999). The charismatic leader has the opportunity to change the status quo, but in the way s/he might offend the employees who worked in the past and contributed to the organization, "the charismatic's verbal messages construct reality such that only the positive features of the future vision and only the negative features of the status quo are emphasized .... What charismatic leaders do is to tie these self-concepts of followers to the goals and collective experiences associated with their missions so that they become valued aspects of the followers' self-concept" (Conger, 1999).

VII. Conclusion

The transformational leader works with the subordinates closely to achieve the goal of the organization. The subordinates share the vision of the leader and they blend their personal goals with the goals of the organization. The transformational leadership is concerned about the relationship between the leader and the followers and to encourage them to reach their maximum potential. The path-goal theory reflects the relationship between the involvement of the leader and the followers. The relationships between charismatic leader and the followers are based on the perception of the leader that the followers have. Not only the perception makes the followers obey the leader but by believing the work is heroic, morally correct, and meaningful. The charismatic leader, unlike the transforming leader, is capable of abusing her/his power. The dark side of the charismatic leadership occurs when the leader takes advantage of the followers' perception of her/his image.

References

Anderson, T. (1992). <u>Transforming leadership: New skills for an extraordinary future.</u> Amherst. Human Development Press, Inc.

Bono, J. & Judge, T. (2003). Self-concordance at work: Toward understanding the motivational effects of transformational leaders. <u>Academy of Management Journal</u>. Vol. 46, Issue 5. Retrieved January 17, 2004 from EBSCOhost website: http://ejournals.ebsco. com/login.asp?bCookiesEnabled=TRUE

Conger, J. (1999). Charismatic and transformational leadership in organizations: An insider's perspective on these developing streams of research. Leadership Quarterly. Vol. 10, Issue 2. Retrieved January 17, 2004 from EBSCOhost website: http://ejournals.ebsco. com/login.asp?bCookiesEnabled=TRUE

House, R. (1996). Path-goal theory of leadership: Lessons, legacy, and a reformulated theory. Leadership Quarterly. Fall96, Vol.7 issue 3, p323, 30p. Retrieved January 5, 2004 from Source http://ejournals. ebsco.com/login.asp?bCookiesEnabled=TRUE

Kuhnert, K & Lewis, P. (1987) Transactional and transformational leadership: A constructive/developmental analysis. Academy of Management. The Academy of Managemet Review. Briarcliff Manor: Vol. 12, Iss. 4; pg 648, 10pgs. Retrieved January 17, 2004 from ProQuest website: http://www.umi.com/proquest/

Pawar, B. & Eastman, K. (1997). The nature and implication of contextual influence on transformational leadership: a conceptual. Academy of Management. Vol. 22, Iss. 1. Retrieved January 17, 2004 from EBSCOhost website: http://ejournals.ebsco.com/login. asp?bCookiesEnabled=TRUE

Schriesheim, C. & Von Glinow, M. (1977). The path-goal theory of leadership: A theoretical and empirical analysis. Academy of Management Journal Vol. 20, No3, 398-405. Retrieved January 3, 2004 from EBSCOhost website: http://ejournals.ebsco.com/login. asp?bCookiesEnabled=TRUE

Waldman, D. & Yammarino, F. (1999). CEO charismatic leadership: Levels-of-management and levels- of analysis effects. <u>Academy of Management. The Academy of Managemet Review.</u> Mississippi State. Vol. 24, Iss. 2; pg 266, 20 pgs. . Retrieved January 17, 2004 from EBSCOhost website: <u>http://ejournals.ebsco.com/login. asp?bCookiesEnabled=TRUE</u>

The International Virtual University

The International Virtual University

I. Thesis

The International Virtual Universities are expanding to include men and women worldwide, all classes of people who will earn higher competitive compensation and who will have better learning satisfaction.

II. Introduction

Literature points out that the International Virtual University (IVU) is an American concern because we do not have a clear picture about the process of the virtual universities and their outcome in the present time and their impact on the future in America. The market share is an indicator of the expansion of the IVU; although, a few universities are dropping or struggling to stay online. There are advantages of the IVU including satisfaction of students with the virtual classroom, and revolutionizing the culture.

III. Literature Review

A. Problems involve the expansion of the virtual university

1. Competing for market share: New York University is dropping the online education

The problem is that a few universities are dropping the online education because of the other competitors or the lack of funding (Gendreau, 2003). If the researcher chooses the survey as a research methodology, the outcome will include positive and negative points of views the participants might express. The data available about the University of Phoenix probably are encouraging but the data about New York University definitely are discouraging (Gendreau, 2003).

2. Established cultures and the virtual university: Culture change and resistance

Many researchers and authors are asking intelligent questions and among them an Economist asked: "What will be the impact of these new information technologies on universities?" (Mehmet, 2002).

The role of the professor is changing as well as is the students' interaction with the professor. The obstacle the students will encounter is their need for access to computers which probably are the main obstacles for students from the Third World (Bates, 1997).

The resistance of the Internet education will occur as a result of the level of risk people are willing to take. The story of Western Universities shows that an International University might suffer setbacks as a result of budget cutbacks, program reduction and declining R & D expenditures (Mehmet, 2002).

B. Advantages of the virtual university worldwide

1. Existence distance education: Indira Gandhi Open University

One million students in China enroll in the Chinese Radio and Television Universities. And more than 100,000 students receive a degree each year from these universities. These universities are called megauniversities. Korea's National Open University and India's Indira Gandhi National Open University are servicing the need for higher education on a global basis (Albrechten, Mariger, & Parker, 2001).

2. Building blocks in human interaction: Higher subjective satisfaction with the virtual classroom

The need for social networks is the building blocks in human interaction regardless of where the members live or work. The relationship people have online is very similar to the traditional relationships offline. The virtual classroom reports higher subjective satisfaction with the virtual classroom than with the traditional classroom (Hiltz and Wellman, 1997).

C. Women issues in remote distances

1. Women forced to live within certain cultures: Indian and Arabian women

Women's role in general in the developing countries has been traditionally suppressed. For example, Indian women and Arabian women are forced to live within certain cultural mores; however, the Internet education would be a breath of fresh air to those women because there is no intellectual distance between men and women (Alder, 1994).

2. Revolutionizing the cultures: Expanding virtual university to include women at a distance

The culture in the developing countries can inhibit women from utilizing their potential. The Internet Virtual University perhaps would revolutionize the culture of these countries. The change probably will be internal and gradual for women to fully examine their potential (Alder, 1994). Online education is important to increase the ability to have access to information, learn new material, and create leaders in the workplace and in life in general.

IV. The Research Design

A. Quantitative research is the research methodology.

B. Surveys are the most suitable quantitative method. University of Phoenix, and City University of Bellevue, Washington, are candidates to provide the help the researcher needs for the surveys created for this research. InfoUSA database company will be able to provide inputs from enrolled senior students who are enrolled at these universities.

C. Hypotheses:

H1, expanding the international virtual university will include all classes of people.

H2, senior students from international virtual universities will expect to earn higher   competitive compensation.

H3, Students at the international virtual universities will have better self-satisfaction   than students who study in a traditional classroom.

D. The surveys

1) The purpose of the surveys is to provide the community the practical picture of the online students and to help the society to understand the depth and the need for educational alternatives for working adults and other classes of people.

2) The survey is the preferred type of data collection because students are spread in a large geographic area. Also, the expected participants are enrolled in the university mentioned above. The sample should not be more than 500 participants to limit the research to a small period of time.

3) The surveys will be cross-sectional with data collected at one point in time.

4) The form of data collection is a self-administrated questionnaire.

5) The population in the study is students at University of Phoenix, and City University. These universities offer distance education and there is a great possibility to collect questionnaires from online senior students who are working on a bachelor degree or a master degree.

6) The sample design for this population is a multistage (clustering) because each university is a different population and the names included in the sample will be obtained from InfoUSA data base company.

7) The sample will be randomly selected.

8) The permission of the universities mentioned above is not crucial.

9) Advanced-notice letter will be sent to the sample participants prior to the actual   surveys.

10) The questions of the surveys will be on Likert scale and open questions.

V. Conclusion

Online education is using the methodology to change the way people are doing business and to change the culture or traditions of the people. The Internet-based education is a new medium for an interactive diversity of people from all over the world. The virtual classroom reports higher subjective satisfaction with the virtual classroom than with the traditional classroom The International Virtual University deals with established cultures and people may be threatened by the education and the new ideology which it brings to the world. Although, the IVU is a remarkable market for advancement the IVU might not reach the majority of student around the globe as a result of the cost and the lack of accessibility of technology.

References

Adler, N. (1994). Competitive frontiers: Women managing across borders. The Journal of Management Development. Bradford: 1994. Vol. 13, Iss. 2; pg. 24, 18 pgs. Retrieved October 13, 2003 from ProQest website: http://www. umi.com/proquest/

Albrechtsen, K., Mariger, H., and Parker, C (2001). Distance education and the impact of technology in Europe and Japan. Educational Technology, Research and Development. Washington: 2001. Vol. 49, Iss. 3; pg. 107, 9 pgs. Retrieved October 13, 2003 from ProQuest website: http://www.umi.com/proquest/

Bates, A. (1997). The impact of technological change on open and distance learning.

Distance Education. Melbourne: 1997. Vol. 18, Iss. 1; pg. 93, 17 pgs. Retrieved October 13, 2003 from ProQuest website: http://www. umi.com/proquest/

Gendreau, R. (2003). What has happened in the business world of on-line distance learning? Journal of American Academy of Business, Cambridge. Hollywood: Mar 2003. Vol. 2, Iss. 2; pg. 467, 5 pgs Retrieved September 30, 2003 from ProQuest website: http://www. umi.com/proquest/

Hiltz, S., & Wellman, B. (1997). Asynchronous learning networks as a virtual classroom. Association for Computing Machinery. Communications of the ACM. New York: Sep 1997. Vol. 40, Iss. 9; pg. 44, 6 pgs. Retrieved October 13,2003 from ProQuest website: http://www.umi.com/proquest/

Mehmet, O (2002). The 'international university' in the age of globalisation: A unifier of knowledge or an Information factory. Humanomics. Patrington: 2002. Vol. 18, Iss. 3/4; pg. 65, 10 pgs. Retrieved October 13, 2003 from ProQuest website: http://www. umi.com/proquest/

Sample for Personal Development

Sample for Personal Development

This essay of my personal development plan consists of descriptions of strengths and opportunities for improvement, weaknesses, and list of specific objectives for learning new behavior patterns. Also it includes my decision of where, when and how to improve my behavior, and finally, to show evidence of my progress. The study is based on the Personal Style Indicator, the Job Style Indicator, Values Performance Indicator, Self Worth Inventory, and the Stress Indicator and the Health Planner which are published by the Consulting Resource Group International, Inc.

According to the Personal Style Indicator, my personal style is a Cognitive/Analysis style. However, my strengths are: acting cautiously to avoid errors, engaging in critical analysis, creating low-stress climate, insuring quality-control, and following directives and standards. Working as an accountant, who performs tax preparation, allows me to be cautious in order to avoid error because one error could cost me money and my reputation. Secondly, after years of experience I am able to understand the tax laws and follow directions and apply standards.

Also, the Personal Style Indicator describes common difficulties and weaknesses for my Cognitive/Analysis style. The difficulties are: getting bogged down in details and losing time, being too critical or finicky, being overly sensitive to feedback and being self-sufficient, alone. Enforcing strengths at work and home would be a good solution, but weaknesses were enforced and repeated in the past as well because of inexperience. For example, being self-sufficient, alone, was the result of lack of references and support in the past, but I ended this weakness by informing the Internal Revenue Service of my desire to list my name in the mailing list to the companies and individuals who were concerned about taxes and accounting. As a result I received a number of names of publishers who publish tax books and offer seminars.

According to the Job Style Indicator, the style of behavior which I think is required in my job as an accountant is Cognitive/Analysis. However, my strengths in handling data are: calculating figures, organizing data, proofreading, maintaining standards, researching, and following instructions. My job demands this behavior. For example, researching is one way to ensure that the financial statements are accurate and the tax forms are prepared according to the standards and the instructions. Also, I would use my strengths to change my career 0 develop critical writing skill with my ability to research and analyze.

My weaknesses are: getting stressed when overworked, asking too many questions, over-reacting when angry, making decisions slowly and being a poor listener. Being a poor listener is the worst behavior I have. I am always feeling threatened by the person who is talking. I get restless from listening especially if I do not agree about what is being said. My mind develops both weakness and strength in what has been said. It doesn't seem logical to me for the speaker to take only one point of view. But these explanations are not enough of an excuse to interrupt the speaker. I have been working on this weakness for a long time and my friends think I have improved.

Values Preference Indicator suggests that my most important values are as follows: independence, spirituality, tranquility, wealth, instruction, intimacy and honesty. The value of independence is very important to me but it is difficult to accomplish. Education is a part of becoming independent considering education leads to financial stability. The decision to be independent is not only based on education but on the choice to be, for example, employee or self-employed. I chose to be self-employed in the field of accounting. As self-employed I also had to obey the client and I didn't have freedom of action. I had chosen to live by the rules and regulations.

Independence is what I value most, and I have to find a way out from the accounting's rules and regulations. Independence is to have freedom of action. However I find freedom in writing and I experience critical writing and research which allow me to develop new ideas and live an active and exciting life. City University introduces me to critical writing which I wish to continue always. It is a way to enhance creativity and expertise which are somewhat important and I would like to have them as very important values to me.

Self Work Inventory helps me to understand my deep bitterness to one of my family members. I was a partner with one of my family but he managed to take over the business for himself, and I was left out to suffer from large losses. My score is medium between 25 and 27 in evaluating myself. I lost my business with this individual 10 years ago but I still suffer the losses. I was surprised because it seemed to me that I would never forget my losses but I think that I overcame the tragedy.

My self-concept and self-esteem are also in the medium range. Difficulties at work and difficulties with some family members lead me to see the negativity and positivity in my self-concept and self-esteem. The time might heal the wounds which I had ten years ago and they could be analyzed in a scientific manner. I study hard to find answers to old questions. Why did my business fail? What is the best way to live and to know howl The Self Worth Inventory evidences that I have improved through the years because I am no longer depressed, but happier, think well of others and evaluate my own performance more positively.

The "Alternatives for Increasing Self-Worth" suggests that I have to develop respect for myself which means that I have to limit or eliminate relationship with negative individuals and that's what I exactly am trying with my previous partner. My relative has a negative influence and mistreats me. Eliminating the relationship is the alternative which I choose to use to forget and to find a way to forgive. And it works.

Stress Indicator and Health Planner indicate that my scores are moderate for Distress Assessment, Interpersonal Stress, and Time Stress Assessment and high score for Wellness and low score for the Occupational Stress Assessment. The low Occupational Stress Assessment's score indicates high stress which is a result of my working environment and the nature of my work. Changing jobs is the most likely to happen. Although I am in a transition to a more challenging and suitable job I try to manage the anxiety which is associated with my current job by listening to soft music, eating healthy food and exercising deep breathing.

In conclusion, despite the fact that my personal style is fit for me working as an accountant, but as Perceptive, I tend to be both critical and creative. This conclusion opens the door for me to continue to write critical reviews hoping to make it in this profession. I should enhance my listening skill and listen more to people. Independence is my first value which I have to be aware. I have to have freedom of action and the critical reviews and case analyses allow me to exercise my freedom.

I am improved over the years because I am happier, think well of others and evaluate my own performance more positively. I manage my anxiety by breathing deeply, listening to some familiar music and eating healthy food. My friends' and my wife's support and opinion are always appreciated because they acknowledge my progress.

Training Within Industries (TWI)

Abstract

TWI programs were associated with high national demand, the high rate of the unemployment, the government, and winning the Second World War.

The methods of investigation are: studying the article's logic and completeness of the authors' argument, analyzing the article's strengths and weaknesses, and supporting fmdings with sources which are cited within the body of the analysis.

Findings revealed that TWI programs lack dealing with human feelings, intentions and interpretations.

Training within Industries

Training, Continuous Improvement, and Human Relations: The U.S. TWI Programs and the Japanese Management Style is an article by Alan G. Robinson and Dean M. Schroeder. The magazine, California Management Review, doesn't give any information about the authors' occupations. The article's issues are: first, the development of the U.S. Training Within Industries ([WI); second, the teaching of the article which assumes that the principles of good management are not as dependent on culture as many might think; third, TWI is a training approach for unemployed people; fourth, the "multiplier effect"; fifth, Job Instruction Training (JIT); sixth, Job Methods Training; seventh, Job Relations Training (JRT).

TWI programs were first introduced to improve the production in the United States to the levels required to win the Second World War. The demand on the defense products was very high and the numbers of unemployed and unskilled people were over eight million U.S. citizens.

After the war Japan was faced with widespread starvation and social disorder. The U.S. occupation authorities thought of TWI programs to be implemented in Japan to boost productivity. However, TWI programs were associated with four factors: first, the high national demand on certain products, such as, tanks and airplanes; second, the high rate of the unemployment; third, the government control; fourth, the vision whether to win a war or to stop the chaotic social disorder in Japan.

The authors argue that TWI "teaches that the principles of good management are not as dependent on culture as many might think" (Robinson and Schroeder, 1993:36). The strength of this statement lies on the concept of active training or training by doing which is referred to Sophocles who lived in 445 BC. But the weakness is that TWI programs consider everybody is alike. The contents of the active training or training by doing are changing; for example, the trainer should collect information about the participants, such as, the nature of the participants' work (or personal) situation, the knowledge, skills, and attitudes of the participants, and the conditions that will affect participant involvement in the training program (Silberman, 1990: 12).

TWI programs were training programs for unemployed people in a certain period of time which was associated with the national demand. However, if the TWI could be taught at any cultural setting, then, TWI programs would work in this decade where the welfare is a significant problem. There is no war or social disorder, there is no national demand on certain items and products in this decade, but there is a stable economy. Technology is changing the people's way of life and training approaches; for example, in this decade "companies hope to use distance learning and multimedia technology to deliver more training and 'just-in-time' information to more workers in more locations efficiently than has ever been possible" (Boling and Sousa, 1993:50).

TWI's multiplier effect is based on a standard method in training people who will train other people who will train groups of people. The trainer has to teach exactly from the manual's instruction, and what to write on the board, and when to write it. TWI programs wanted people to do what they were told. But what TWI and other organizations "do not do is get people to reflect on their work and behavior" (Argyris, 1994: 77). TWI programs end by training groups, usually a group of 12 persons each. Learning about group dynamics is missing in TWI programs. On the other hand, active training which promotes learning by doing, illustrates six major experiential learning approaches which are role playing, games and simulations, observation, mental imagery, write tasks, and projects (Silberman, 1990) which all are missing in TWI.

The article succeeded to explain the result of the Job Instruction Training (JIT). The increase in the nation's airplane production, tank production and the gunpowder, according to the article, was a result of U.S. booming business for its defense contractors. But the article doesn't answer its question, that is "if the TWI programs were so good, why did they die out in the United States after W orld War II" (Robinson & Schroeder, 1993: 55). Also the article doesn't explain how the U.S. will implement TWI in this decade which is known by its technology, communication superhighway, and information. Training and learning should be changed because "we will all become the 'six million dollar man', hooked to global telecommunications -- once the price comes down" (Glenn, 1993:44). However, this advanced technology will "link our bodies with the rest of the world for thought and action" (Glenn, 1993:48).

In Job Methods Training (JMT), the fIrst TWI step is to break down the job into its constituent operations, that is, move inspection and delay. Break down the job into its consituent operations is based on the principles of Scientific Management which is criticized by many scholars. As an example, Peter M. Senge promotes system thinking and once he said that "we are literally killing ourselves because of our inability to understand wholes" (Galagan, 1991: 5). The TWI programs lacks dealing with human feelings, intentions, and interpretations. TWI is the beginning of machine-like human. During the war the government had no choice but to teach a tough training program. It might be the time for the organizations to take responsibility to train people (Avishai, 1994).

TWI programs were associated with the high national demand, the high rate of the unemployment, and to win WWII. The contents of the training by doing changed over the years. Technology is changing people's way of life, and distance learning is a new way of life. TWI lacks learning group dynamics and experiental learning. TWI programs lack dealing with human feelings, intentions and interpretations. The organizations, not the government, should take responsibility to train people.

Annotated Bibliography

Argyris, C. (1994). Good communication that blocks learning. <u>Harvard Business Review</u>. JulyAug.: 77-85 Rosdale Public Library, Baltimore, MD. The author argues that what companies do not do is get peaple to reflect on their work and behavior.

Avishai, B. (1994). What is business social compact. <u>Harvard Business Review</u>. Jan.-Feb.: 38-48 Rosdale Public Library, Baltimore, MD The author argues that the organizations should take responsibility to train people.

Bolling,E. & Sousa, G. A. (1993). Interface Design issues in the future of business training <u>Business Horizons</u>. Nov.-Des.: 50-54 Enoch Public Library, Baltimore MD. The author argues that companies hope to use distance learning and multimedia ; technology to deliver more training.

Galagan, P. A. (1991). The Learning organization made plain. <u>Training and development.</u> Oct.: p37(8) WOW Station, Northpoint Public Library, Baltimore, MD. The author argues that Peter Senge said that we are literally killing ourselves because of our inability to understand wholes.

Glenn, J.C. (1993). The Post information age: new horizons for business and education. Nov.-Des.: 44-49 Enoch Public Library, Baltimore, MD. He argues that we will link our bodies with the rest of the world for thought and action.

Silberman, M. (1990). Active Training. Lexington Books, An Imprint of Macmillan, N.Y. City University Bookstore, Renton, WA. The author argues that the trainer has to collect information about each participant.

The Training Project

The Training Project

The goals of this analysis are to clarify my training project's objectives, to use the Action Research Model, to apply the Adult Learning Model, to provide elements that appeal to various learning styles, and to critique the participants' feedback. On the other hand, this analysis answers questions, such as, to what extent were my training goals achieved; in what ways did I adapt to participants feedback during the training; and what observations do I have regarding the feedback I received from the group.

There were two types of objectives I tried to accomplish in my training project. The first groups of objectives were to be able to train the participants by using an alternative method to lecturing. I chose Read and Discuss method. I decided to modify this method to fit some participants who refused to read and preferred to listen. I planned to lead discussion after reading few statements, but the discussion was dominated by one participant the most of the time. I used the Beer

Game, as an opening to my training project, to gain my audience's interest and I used examples from real life to maximize understanding. The second groups of objectives were the training subject itself, to train the participants the meaning of system thinking and to understand wholes.

The Action Research Model was used as background in my training project. The relationship between the participants and I was well established. I collected data about my participants and I got clear consensus about their training needs. The training was conducted at one of the participant's house. I failed to share with the group my training plan before conducting the training class. I didn't involve them before the meeting because I thought that my knowledge about them was enough for me to have their attention. The subject actually surprised some of them. Because the participants were from different businesses the Action Research Model wasn't Applied literally.

I was able to apply the Adult Learning Model. I discussed the participants experiences which they shared with me; although, the participants were still under the influence of the beer game. I was able to have them look to their recent way of thinking and to have alternatives which were explained and emphasized during the training, to distinguish between system thinking and the participant's thinking, and to realize wholes as another way to solve problems. I failed to find general trends and truths in the experiences that participants have had already and to form

I used the Assessment sheet for each participant as a tool for feedback. One member of the group couldn't distinguish between her thinking and system thinking because it is due to her long employment years and as a part of a rigid system at a national company, and the difficulty of the concept. Another participant wasn't able to understand "wholes" because he was trapped in the beer game's details. This participant, as I understood from my previous interaction with him, had tendency to pay attention to small details and he forgot the big picture. The third participant and the cameraperson was able to comprehend the subject, although, she was only listening.

I had two types of objectives to conduct my training project. First group of objectives were to choose read and discuss method, to modify read and discuss method to fit the trainees, and to use the beer game to gain the group's interest. The second groups of objectives were the training subject itself. My relationship between the group and I was well established. The Action Research Model wasn't applied literally because the participants were from different businesses. I failed to find general trends and truths in the experiences that participants have had already. I used the assessment sheets for each participant as a tool for feedback.

Assessment Sheet   Yes   No

Did you understand the concept of
"system thinking"?   _____ _____

Can you distinguish between your
thinking and system thinking?   _____ _____

Will you be able to apply "system
thinking" at your work, home, or church?   _____ _____

Will you be able to modify your old
behaviors and test new behaviors?   _____ _____

Will you be able to understand wholes?   _____ _____

Was the training program successful?   _____ _____

Do you know you are not the person
you used to be seven years ago   _____ _____

Empowerment

Abstract

Empowerment is ownership and responsibility for solving problems and continuation of commitment. The relationship between bosses and subordinates should be more entrepreneurial and empowered in both ways of the ladder and within partnership.

The methods of investigation are: studying the article's logic and completeness of the author's argument, analyzing the article's strengths and weakness, and supporting findings with sources which are cited within the body of the analysis.

Findings revealed that organizations measure success and achievement by standards and benchmarks which eliminate the managers' and subordinates' burden of bureaucracy and control. Inspiration, creativity and motivation are personal powers which are held by everyone. Subordinates are trustworthy and should be treated as equal partners.

Empowerment

Control in an Age of Empowerment is an article by Robert Simons. Mr. Simons is the Charles M. Williams Professor of Business Administration at Harvard Business School in Boston, Massachusetts. He is the author of Levers of Control: How Managers Use Innovation Control Systems to Drive Strategic Renewal, which was published in December 1994 by the Harvard Business School Press. This article is relevant to this course because it sheds light on the leadership and stewardship philosophies and the dilemma which arises from applying those philosophies in the 1990's relating to empowerment versus control in the work place. The article's issues, managers attempting to harness the creativity of employee, are: First, diagnostic control systems; second, beliefs systems; third, boundary systems; and fourth, the interactive control systems.

The article defines empowerment as an attempt "to harness the creativity of employees" (Simons, 1995: 81). This definition is well known in the business world; for example, other sources define empowerment as to give" employees jobs and freedom they need to be creative while doing them" (Snyder and Graves, 1994: 1). But what if the job requires no creativity; for instance, data entry jobs which are based on canned programs which allow the employee no creativity; or what if the employee himself is not creative and he likes to do routine work, then creativity is not the perfect definition for empowerment. However, empowerment is understood best as "the act of standing on our own ground, discovering our own voice, making our own choice" and "taking responsibility" are "at the heart of claiming our freedom" (Block, 1993: 36).

The article claims that four systems of control are equally important in today's business environment. The article actually shifts a direct control as "machinelike bureaucracies" (Simons, 1995: 80) to an indirect control. "Control means that there is a clear line of authority, and ... people, at the middle and the bottom, exist to execute and implement" (Block, 1993: 23); however, the article suggests that people in the middle and the bottom should be empowered but they have to be inside four systems of control. The article suggests that "managers who use their missions as living documents - as part of a system to guide patterns of acceptable behavior have discovered a powerful lever of control" (Simons, 1995: 82) which means that the relationship, in an organization, is still a top-down relationship. It seems that the article agrees with the "people" who "behave as if their bosses were not very dependent on them" (Gabarro & Kotter, 1993: 151) because the relationship in the work place should be both ways, top-down and bottom-up "partnership" (Block, 1993: 23).

The article emphasizes four control systems to achieve creativity. The article doesn't promote responsibility ownership, but for the sake of creativity, people should be under a sort of control or disguised control. "Traditional management has embraced a controlling philosophy" Hegarty, 1993: 3) which is embraced by the article and considered it as a solution for the failure of the organic structure that is adopted by today's organizations. As soon as people at the top, in all good faith, devise ways of controlling and motivating their workforce, time will have passed and ownership and commitment will have to be persuaded, bought, or demanded (Block, 1993: 25).

Organizations measure success and achievement by standards and benchmarks. The article claims that "diagnostic control systems are not adequate to ensure effective control," (Simon, 1995: 81) but the article switches, all of the sudden, to diagnostic measurement systems and it states that "one of the main purposes of diagnostic measurement systems is to eliminate the manager's burden of constant monitoring" (Simons, 1995: 82). Diagnostic control systems, in the article's point of view, help managers to track the progress of the individual toward important goals, but diagnostic measurement systems mean that once goals are established, employees will be working diligently to meet the agreed-upon goals and many managers believe they can move on to other issues (Simons, 1995). However, the article doesn't explain which diagnostic it promotes because they are two different diagnostic systems.

The article articulates the four systems as tools for managers to control. The article ignores the personality of the individuals. Taking risk, for instance, might not be the result of a system but might be the personality. "From my observations, the reason one individual seeks risks while another approaches the problem conservatively depends more on his or her personality" (Zaleznik, 1992: 129). Even establishing boundary systems, the article limits the workforce's contribution by telling them what they should and shouldn't do. Someone who knows best at the top is always there in every organization to exercise his or her beliefs, to document them, and to enforce them on the rest of the organization in spite of the significant differences and diversities among the organization's members. Again "of all beliefs that to inspire performance, the most essential one is a sense of personal power, which is held by every person within the organization" (Adams, et al, 1993: 99).

In contrast, people who are on their own to connect their culture might be wrong because "when people are left on their own to make the connections, they sometimes create very inaccurate links" (Kotter, 1995: 67), which is consistent with the idea behind each of the four systems. Because the article claims that "empowerment is fueled by inspiration and performance rewards it should never be interpreted as giving subordinates a blank check" (Simons, 1995: 84). Thus, it means that top managers shouldn't trust those subordinates.

Empowerment is ownership and responsibility for solving problems and continuation of commitment. The relationship between bosses and subordinates should be more entrepreneurial and empowered both ways and within a partnership. Organic structure of the organizations of the 1990's and the humanistic relationship which is based on the reality of the workforce's diversity are the best suited for the organization of tomorrow. Organizations measure success and achievement by standards and benchmarks which eliminate the manager's and subordinate's burden of bureaucracy and control. Inspiration, creativity and motivation are personal powers which are held by everyone. Subordinates are trustworthy and should be treated as equal partners.

Annotated Bibliography

Adams, J. D. et. al. (1993). Transforming Leadership. From Vision To Results. A Miles River Press, Alexandria, VA. City University Bookstore, Renton, W A. The authors argue that the most essential belief is the personal power which is held by everyone within the organization.

Block, P. (1993). Stewardship, Choosing Service Over Self-Interest. Berrett-Koehler Pubishers, San Francisco, CA. City University Bookstore, Renton, W A. The author argues that as soon as people at the top, in all good faith, devise ways of controlling and motivating their workforce, time will have passed and ownership and commitment will have to be persuaded, bought, or demanded.

Gabarro, J. J. & J. P. Kotter (1993). Managing your boss. Harvard Business Review.

May-June: 150-157, North Point Public Library, Baltimore, MD. The authors argue that people should know that top management depend on them as

Hegarty, W. H. (1993). Organizational survival means embracing change. Business Horizons, Nov.-Dec.: p1(4). WOW Station of North Point Public Library, Baltimore, MD. The author argues that traditional management has embraced a controlling philosophy.

Kotter, J. P. (1995). Leading change: why transformation efforts fail. Harvard Business Review. March-April: 59-67. North Point Public Library, Baltimore, MD. The author argues that when people are left on their own to make the connection, they sometimes create very inaccurate links.

Snyder, N. H. & Graves, M. (1994). Leadership and vision. importance of goals and . objectives in leadership. Business Horizons. Jan.-Feb.: pI (6). WOW Station of North Point Public Library, Baltimore, MD. They argue that empowerment is to give employees jobs and freedom they need to be creative while doing them.

Zaleznik, A. (1992). Managers and leaders: are they different. <u>Harvard Business Review.</u> March-April: 126-135. North Point Public Library, Baltimore, MD. The author argues that from his observations, the reason one individual seeks risk while another approaches the problem conservatively depends more on his or her personality.

Corporate Debt and the Investment Opportunities

Abstract

The stockholders should be aware of the firm's protection against takeover and the bondholders' priority. There is no clear cut of correlation between the size of the firm, the regulation, and the level of debt.

The methods of investigation are: studying the article's logic and completeness of the author's argument, analyzing the article's strengths and weaknesses, and supporting findings with sources which are cited within the body of the analysis.

Findings revealed that bond value itself changes over time and affect the debt maturity choice. There is no evidence that large size firms which issue long term bonds are low quality firms.

Corporate Debt and the Investment Opportunities

The Maturity Structure of Corporate Debt is an article by Michael 1. Barclay and Clifford W. Smith, Jr. Barclay and Smith are from the William E. Simon Graduate School of Business Administration, University of Rochester, New York. The article is appropriate to this book because it sheds light on the corporate debts as a capital source which involves the firm's capital components and costs. The article explains the incentives that lead large public corporations to choose particular financing policies. The article's issues are: first, the theory of debt maturity; second, measuring debt maturity; third, the determination of debt maturity structure; fourth, investment opportunity set, scale economies, public debt and commercial paper.

The article's weaknesses lie in the analysis of the corporations' future investment opportunities. The article claims that "In some cases, bondholders capture enough of the profits so that a profitable project does not offer stockholders a normal return," (Barclay and Smith, 1995: 610) but the article does not explain what is the normal return. It is obvious that the investor should be aware of the priority of bonds when it comes to payout. Even when the bonds carry a contractual innovation; such as, "Poison puts" (Cook and Easterwood, 1994: 1905) bonds are still considered debt and they have to be paid first. Poison puts actually "make firms less attractive as takeover targets and thus provide an additional mechanism for strengthening managerial resistance to hostile bids." (Cook & Easterwood, 1994: 1906). The stockholders should be aware of the bondholders' priority.

The article builds its hypothesis on the assumption that "regulated fIrms will have longer-maturity debt than unregulated firms" (Barclay and Smith, 1995: 612); however, this assumption is in line with the findings of another article which claims that "at least 70 percent of our firms decrease their leverage ratios after privatization" (Megginson, Mash, & Randenborgh, 1994, 104: 11-12). But the article doesn't explain what if the regulated firms are small firms. The article argues that "Firm size is potentially correlated with debt maturity;" for example, "Small firms ... choose bank debt over public debt" (Barclay & Smith, 1995: 612). But what, as I mentioned previously, if the small fiIm is also regulated.

The article does not explain the impact of highly leveraged firms on the market. The size as the article claims is correlated with debt maturity; but if those firms are highly leveraged, does that mean "highly leveraged firms lose market share to their less leveraged competitors in industry downturns" (Opler and Titman, 1994: 8). Furthermore, the article does not provide enough evidence of the correlation between the size, the degree of debt, and the regulation. And it does not mention the cost of debt for different maturities. The cost of capital, and especially the cost of debt, is important for budgeting decisions for maximizing the value of the firm by minimizing the cost of debt (Brigham & Gapenski, 1994: 334).

The article assumes that "firms with high dividend yield ten to have more long term debt" (Barclay & Smith, 1995: 623). On the other hand, "bond prices decline when dividends are increased" and "bond prices increase when dividends decrease" (Dhillon & Johnson, 1994: 288). In other words, the article assumes that firms will have more long-term debt if the stock prices are dropped. It is consistent with the concept which argues that firms sell bonds above par or at a premium when dividends decrease. Also, the bond value itself changes over time and the article fails to explain its affect on the debt maturity choice (Brigham & Gapenski, 1994: 282).

The article discusses an enlightening idea which is the firm quality. The article speaks to the investor, and teaches him or her, a lesson in finance and how to recognize and distinguish between corporations. The article emphasizes and agrees that "high quality firms will issue more short-term debt and low quality firms will issue more long term-debt" (Barclay & Smith, 1995: 613). But this idea is demolished when the article claims that the firm size is correlated with the debt maturity. If a large size firm issues long-term debt then the large size firm is only a low quality firm. And a high quality firm is a small firm which is less able to take advantage of the scale economies. On the other hand, bond value depends on the dollar of interest paid multiplied by PVIFA plus the par value of the bond multiplied by PVIF (Brigham and Gapenski, 1994: 282).

The article "indicates that non-rated firms (which tend to be small firms with lowest credit standing) have more short-term debt." (Barclay & Smith, 1995: 627). The article goes fmther and suggests that there is a non-monotonic relation between credit standing and debt maturity, and it is convincing. But if there is a relationship between credit and debt maturity why hasn't the article explained the risk of short-term debt and the lender's reluctance to refinance the debt if bad news arrives. There are a number of reasons that short-term debt could be a disadvantage for small or large firms; for example, a short-term debt is subject to more random disturbance than long-term debt, and they are relatively exposed to high degree of reinvestment rate risk. (Brigham & Gapenski, 194: 342).

Bonds are still considered debt and they have to be paid first. In some cases stockholders should be aware of the firm protection against takeover and the bondholders' priority. Regulated firms are not necessarily large size firms. It might be a correlation between the size, the regulation and the degree or level of debt which the article doesn't explain. There is need for explanation about the cost of debt for different maturities. The bond value itself change over time and affect the debt maturity choice. As a result of a careful investigation it isn't clear that large size firms which issue long-term bonds should be labeled low quality firms. There are a number of reasons the short-term debt could be a disadvantage for small [ums but it is accessible for small firms which are not necessarily with lowest credit standing.

Annotated Bibliography

Brigham, E. F. & Gapenski, L.C. (1994). <u>Financial Management -</u> <u>Theory and Practice</u>. The Dryden Press, Fort Worth, TX. City University Bookstore, Renton, W A. The authors argue that the cost of capital is important for budgeting decisions for maximizing the value of the firm by <u>minimizing</u> the cost of capital.

Cook, D. O. & Easterwood, J. C. (1994). Poison put bonds: an analysis of their economic role.

<u>The Journal of Finance</u>. December: 1905-1920, Enoch Pratt Public Library, Baltimore, The authors argue that bonds carry a contractual innovation; such as, poison puts are still considered debt and they have to be paid frrst.

Dhillon, U. S. & Johnson, H. (1994). The Effect of dividend change on stock and bond prices.

The Journal of Finance. March: 281-289, Enoch Pratt Public Library, Baltimore, MD. The authors argue that bond prices decline when dividends are increased and bond prices

Megginson, W. L., et al (1994). The Financial and operating performance of newly privatized frrms: an international empirical analysis. The Journal of Finance. June: p 403(50), WOW Station of North Point Public Library, Baltimore, MD. The author argues that 70% of our firms decrease their leverage ratio after privatization.

Opler, T. C. & Titman, S. (1994). Financial distress and corporate performance. The Journal of Finance. July: p 1015(26), WOW Station of North Point Public Library, Baltimore MD. The authors argue that highly leveraged firms lose market share to their less leverage competitors in industry downturn.

Total Quality Management

Abstract

Learning is the heart of Total Quality Management (TQM). Organizations should implement TQM to become World-Class organizations. The organization should plan total quality management, including learning, side-by-side with the organization's overall plan. World-Class organizations are the product of continuous implementation of TQM's principles and philosophy.

Total Quality Management

This critical review analyzes the article, "New Paradigm Organizations: From Total Quality to Learning to World-Class," by Richard M. Hodgetts, Fred Luthans and Sang M. Lee. Richard M. Hodgetts is a professor of management at Florida International University, and he is the author or co-author of 22 hardcover texts. Fred Luthans is the George Holmes Distinguished Professor of Management at the University of Nebraska, Lincoln, and editor of Organizational Dynamics. He published a number of major books. And finally, Sang M. Lee is a university eminent scholar and distinguished professor. He is the director of the Center for Technology Management and Decision Science at the University of Nebraska, Lincoln. The article claims that Total Quality Management is the first stage for the organizations to compete globally.

The authors claim that the purpose from their article is the "Organization design has entered a new paradigm - an area of new rules, new boundaries, and new ways of behaving ... (and) to examine the new paradigm organizations: total quality, learning and world-class" (Hodgetts, et aI, 1994:5). The authors' ideas are not new to the masters of Total Quality Management. For example, the article says 10 core values are generally recognized as total quality characteristics: 1) Customer driven, 2) Leadership, 3) Full participation, 4) Reward system, 5) Reduce cycle time, 6) Prevention, not detection, 7) Management by fact, 8) Long range outlook, 9) Partnership development, and 10) Public responsibility (Hodgetts, et aI, 1994: 6-7).

These previous characteristics are the foundation of quality management as they are described by the masters; such as, Philip Crosby, W. Edwards Deming, and Joseph M. Juran (Brocka & Brocka, 1992: 61-104). The article states that, "Top management involvement often begins with senior-level executives" (Hodgetts, et aI, 1994: 8); although, this is not often the rule because "Departmental and divisional managers have often been the initiators" (Grant, et aI, 1994:27). On the other hand, the article describes planning and organizing the effort to implement quality management by realistic experiences of several companies; such as, Marlow Industries, a 1991 Baldrige Winner, who has created a Total Quality Management Council (Hodgetts, et aI, 1994: 10)

The article states that there is a "Fine line between total quality organization and learning organization - a critical step toward becoming a world-class organization" (Hodgetts, et aI, 1994:11). The article distinguishes learning process from total quality management despite the fact that learning is the heart of TQM. Learning according to the article is reflected by the experience of "Companies; such as, Motorola, Zytec and Toyota (which) have moved from a total quality approach to a learning approach because they not only adapt to change, but learn to stay ahead of change" (Hodgetts, et al, 1994: 12), which is "The idea behind continuous improvement, or Kaizen" (Brocka & Brocka, 1992:11) the center point of Total Quality Management.

The basic techniques in the TQM are used in learning organizations; such as, group cause-effect and quality costs. But the article adds other techniques, which are dialogue, scenario analysis, and process reengineering; although, reengineering is the name given to a new combination of techniques that have been used for many years, especially in rapidly changing fields. TQM is based on broad organizational participation to make gradual enhancements to products and services for customers and suppliers, reengineering, therefore, allows for radical changes in organizational structure to make quantum leaps in performance (Forbes, 1994:471). In other words, reengineering process is a well known process to TQM.

The article states that a World-Class organization is an organization's status. Also, the "World-Class organizations include total quality, learning organizational characteristics, and more" (Hodgetts, et al, 1994:14). The article argues that World- Class organization is a status which is reached by customer-base focused to meet customer needs, shared vision, ownership of tasks and solutions, empower teams for generating new ideas, and rewarding employees for excellent service to customer (Hodgetts, et al, 1994: 14-15). These ideas are not beyond Total Quality Management, but the bottom line in TQM. The article's classification of the organization to total quality, learning, and world- class reflects misunderstanding of TQM because they are three dimensions to TQM.

Juran's approach to quality planning includes customer-based focus as a backbone of TQM. Juran's approach states: 1) Identify customer, 2) Determine the customers' needs, 3) Create product features which can meet the customers' needs. Juran also includes in his approach to quality improvement that managers should revise the reward system to enforce the rate of improvement (Brocka & Brocka, 1992:80-84). The article argues that "A distinctive characteristic of world-class organizations is that they continuously improve what they do" (Hodgetts, et al, 1994: 15). This previous concept is taken from quality management principle or Kaizen as the Japanese call it (Brocka & Brocka, 1992:11).

"For world-class organizations, however, constant training has emerged as a particularly important element. To equip employees to fully use their creativity and innovative ideas on the job, the managers and the employees must be effectively trained (Hodgetts, et al, 1994: 17). The key word in this quotation is training, and the key word for

TQM is also training human resources at all levels (Brocka & Brocka, 1992:83).

The article's classification of the organization paradigm: total quality, learning, and world-class is necessary to explain Total Quality Management. TQM principles and philosophy are tools to reach the world-class organization as sailboats aligned and heading toward a sun labeled "World-Class." (George, 1992: 6). There is no fine line between the total quality and learning, and the world-class organization. The fact is that organizations should implement total quality which includes learning and continues improvement to become world-class in a competitive and changing world.

Annotated Bibliography

Brocka B., & Brocka, M. S. (1992). Quality Management. Richard D. Irwin, Inc., New York, NY, City University Bookstore, Belevue, W A. The authors argue that the continuous improvement is the center point of total quality management.

Forbes, L. H. (1994). What do you do when your organization isn't ready for tqm. National Productivity Review. 33: 467-478, City University Library, Renton, W A. He argues that TQM is based on broad organizational partipation to make gradual enhancements to products and services for customers and suppliers.

George, S. (1992). The Baldrige Quality System. John Wiley & Sons, Inc., New York, NY, City University Bookstore, Bellevue, W A. The author argues that total quality, learning is the process which leads to a world-class organization that is able to compete globally.

Hodgetts, R. M., et al. (1994). New paradigm organizations: from total quality to learning to world-class. <u>Organizational Dynamics</u>. 22: 5-19. City University Library,

Renton, W A. The authors argue that organization design has entered a new paradigm: total quality, learning, and world-class.

Transforming Leadership

Abstract

Organic and mechanistic structures are exchangeable structures or incorporated. Transforming leadership should be considered. Mutual respect should be the rule between groups or classes.

The methods of investigation are: to state issues relevant to the course content, to analyze the logical analysis of the author's presentation, to analyze the article's strengths and weaknesses, and to state the logical basis for agreement and disagreement.

Findings revealed that there are several techniques to deal with the organization's boundaries and conflict.

Transforming Leadership

The New Boundaries of the "Boundaryless" Company is an article by Larry Hirschhorn and Thomas Gilmore. Larry Hirschhorn is a principal of the Wharton Center for Applied Research in Philadelphia. Hirschhorn's most recent book is Managing in the New Team Environment: Skills, Tools, and Methods. Thomas Gilmore is the Wharton Center's vice president and he is the author of Making a Leadership Change: How Organizations and Leaders Can Handle Leadership Transitions Successfully. The article claims: First, the organizations become more organic, and the traditional organizational map describes a world that no longer exists. Second, organizations' boundaries are in the mind of managers and employees. Third, companies blur their traditional boundaries to respond to the new technologies, fast-changing markets, and global competition. Fourth, the stronger the negative feelings people have about work interaction, the more likely they are a symptom of a real organizational problem.

The article states, "The problem is that this traditional organizational map describes a world that no longer exists" (Hirschhorn & Gilmore, 1992: 105). The article means that mechanistic, and rigid structure belong to a world that no longer exists. On the other hand, the text book by Richard L. Daft argues that mechanistic and organic structures are exchangeable management structures. The textbook goes one step further and states that, "The organization can behave in an organic way when the situation calls for the initiation of new ideas and in a mechanistic way to implement and use the ideas" (Daft, 1993: 257). In other words, the organic structure can generate innovative ideas but is not the best structure for using those ideas (Daft, 1993: 257). Therefore, the need for mechanistic structure rises as another way to implement the new ideas. Although organic and mechanistic structures could be incorporated as to give the employees the freedom to improve their job but they also have to work hard at their jobs, to give them freedom to meet in groups away from the shop floor, to be creative and innovative, and to work hard in the shop floor to implement those ideas (Daft, 1993: 257).

The article claims that organizations' boundaries are in the mind of managers and employees. The article also argues that "Once traditional boundaries of hierarchy, function, and geography disappear, a new set of boundaries becomes important" (Hirschhorn & Gilmore, 1992: 105). Those new boundaries are "authority" boundaries, the "task" boundaries, the "political" boundaries, and the "identity" boundaries. There is no difference between the traditional hierarchy boundary and the new authority boundary. The article doesn't provide enough evidence to distinguish the traditional hierarchy boundary and the new authority boundary. The article states that, "Even in the most boundaryless company (organic and flexible company) some people lead and others follow, some provide direction while others have responsibility for execution" (Hirschhorn & Gilmore, 1992: 107). On the other hand, in more flexible organizations, "Managers need to take charge and to provide strong leadership" (Hirschhorn & Gilmore, 1992: 107), then it is not a psychological boundary but it is a leadership issue. The article doesn't state the psychological impact which is associated with the boundaryless company. The article, for example, doesn't answer questions; such as, does the boundaryless and flexible company cause psychological disorder to the employees or to the managers because of its horizontal structure? How do they behave? Are they behaving differently than people who work in a traditional structure? Psychology is defined as, 'The science that studies behavior and mental process" (Atkinson et aI, 1987: 674).

The article identifies the identity boundary and argues that, "When people begin to think in terms of 'us' versus 'them' of their in-group as opposed to other out-groups, they are engaged in a relationship at the identity boundary" (Hirschhorn & Gilmore, 1992: 109). However, the article states logical definition about the identity boundary. The definition concludes any group versus any group, generalizing this fact. But the article, without a good reason, seems to undermine shop- floor workers when it states that, "sometimes these identities are a product of a particular occupational or professional culture: attorneys, engineers, software programmers, even shop-floor workers," (Hirschhorn & Gilmore, 1992: 109) by using word "even" to include shop-floor workers with the other occupations or professions. The article describes and analyzes the psychological boundaries between the engineers and the workers, but what about the article's authors-workers relationship; are there psychological boundaries between themselves and the workers. Are the authors of article victims of the psychological boundaries?

The article claims that teams bring people with different but complementary skills together and tie them to a single goal. The article argues that teams are the solution in more specialized work because specialized work makes it harder for people to have a common mission (Hirschhorn & Gilmore, 1992: 108). But because "The external environment is complex and rapidly changing, the organizational departments become highly specialized to handle the uncertainty in their external sector" (Daft, 1993: 81). However, teams are a technique for managing conflict among groups but there are other techniques which provide better approaches for managing conflicts between people with different but complementary skills. The first technique would be structural separation which means separating the conflict departments physically. Second, bureaucratic authority which means senior management invokes rules to resolve a conflict. Third, integration devices; as such as teams or task forces that span the boundary among departments (Daft, 1993: 445-446). Therefore, if the task boundary, as the article is claiming, is a psychological boundary in a flexible structure then the solution would be a traditional one.

The article claims that companies blur their traditional boundaries to respond to the new technologies, fast-changing markets, and global competition. The article describes the mechanistic organizations as traditional organizations which no longer exists. Also the same article states that, "Just because work roles are no longer defined by the formal organizational structure doesn't mean that differences in authority, skill, talent, and perspective simply disappear" (Hirschhorn & Gilmore, 1992: 105). It seems that in the external environment, the tax laws for example, forces the tax firm to be mechanistic. The tax firm is using tax software which is written very carefully to apply the most detail in the tax law. However, the tax firm depends mostly on new technologies; such as, software which should be rigid in applying the law. The impact of the external authority is powerful over a company such as a tax firm. However, the inconsistency of the article shows the reality which cannot be denied. The reality which allows companies to be mechanistic or organic or both respond to different situations.

The article argues that the stronger the negative feelings people have about work interaction, the more likely they are a symptom of a real organizational problem. The article describes the workers' feelings about the engineer and says, "The worker has focused on the task. And he wants to be the engineer's colleague" (Hirschhorn & Gilmore, 1992: 106). The article touches the organization or perhaps the society's structure which is known to the western block. Specializing creates groups and classes of people who are associated with each other. The trend of this article is to stabilize diversity. But the identity boundary which is mentioned in the article is usually formed even in small groups. "Group sameness" is an example of being related to one class or group of people and it is the origin of the society. The negative feelings people have about work interaction, the article argues, is a result of being related to a certain group. To solve diversity boundaries is not to dissolve classes or groups of people but the solution is to have mutual respect for each other. However, the article states that creating and supporting team spirit without devaluing the potential contribution of other groups is the real challenge of work at the identity boundary (Hirschhorn & Gilmore, 1992: 109).

Organic and mechanistic structures are exchangeable structures or incorporated. Managers need to take charge and emphasize leadership issues. Shop- floor workers should be treated with respect and dignity. Managing boundaries is not solely group technique but there are several techniques which provide ways to deal with conflicts; such as, structural separation, bureaucratic authority and integration devices. To solve diversity boundaries is not to dissolve groups of people - the solution is to have mutual respect for each other.

Annotated Bibliography

Atkinson, R. L. et al (1987). <u>Introduction to Psychology</u>. Harcourt Brace Jovanovich, Publishers. New York, NY. Liberty University, Lynchburg, VA. The authors defme Psychology as the science that studies behavior and mental process.

Daft, R. L. (1992). <u>Organization Theory and Design</u>. West Publishing Company, 31. Paul, MN. City University Bookstore, Renton, WA. The organization can behave in an organic way when the situation calls for the initiation of new ideas and in a mechanistic way to implement and use the ideas.

Hirschhorn L. & Gilmore, T. (1992). The New boundaries of the "boundaryless" company.

<u>Harvard Business Review</u>. July-August: 1 04-115. North Point Public Library, Baltimore, MD.

Studying Cultural Differences

Abstract

The concept of high and low context cultures narrows the classifications of people to create specifications of stereotypes. Studying cultural differences is important because it influences the individual communicating ability.

Studying Cultural Differences

The article, Put diversity in Context by Jim Kennedy and Anna Everest (1991) claims that people are divided into high and low context classifications. The supervisor and managers have to become aware of the differences between people's background cultures and their different ways of communicating. The article also claims that only high context cultures value harmony; but in fact, harmony exists in low context cultures as well. The article also ignores the a fundamental similarity exists between the groups. Emphasizing similarity would overcome the cultural differences. The article gives insight and new understanding to the field of communication.

The article is important of leaders and mangers, especially in the United States because American people are from different nationalities, races, religions, and of course genders. Americans are keeping the records of any change of the country's structures. Statistics are well prepared to measure the number of different cultures, and it seems that this is the time to manage diversity and cultural differences in America. "Even if a person is fluent in English is doesn't mean that he or she also is fluent in the American culture" (Kennedy and Everest, 1991). It is true that the majority of American people speak the English language, but they are a multicultural society and "We have to overcome language and stereotype barriers" (Harris & Moran, 1991) and the culture differences. Studying culture is important because it influences the individual's communications and the leadership style.

The article divides human's culture around the globe into high and low context classifications. It is illogical to divide around three billion people simply into either low or high contexts. Egypt, for example, is considered a homogeneous country, but it is divided into many cultures. For instance, there is the different culture between the north and the south of Egypt, the religious differences, the Arab and the Coptic differences, and even each class of people has a different cultural behavior. There are also the cultural differences between generations and eras to consider. The article seems to narrow the classification of people to create specific stereotypes.

An organization's culture is established and the individual should adopt the organization's culture. The components of an organization's culture are values, rites and rituals, heroes and communication, norms, stories, and climate (O'Hair & Fredrich, 1992). All members of the organization should work in harmony. "People from high context cultures see themselves primarily as members of a group" (Kennedy and Everest, 1991); however, if high context cultures value harmony in group then organization in low context culture countries have to become high context culture organizations.

"Not long ago, the term 'work force' conjured up images of white men in ties or blue collars. Today employers must increasingly look to women and minorities. Between now and the year 2000, Blacks and Hispanics will account for 50% of all labor force growth" (Hewlett, 1991). In other words, "The new people coming into our work force are high context, yet most members of management are medium/low context" (Kennedy & Everest, 1991). Accepting cultural diversities would spot differences, but also it should contribute to human species the discovery of the cultural similarity. Such similarity is human instinct motivation to aacomplish his or her goals without breaking laws as an expression of his or her harmony in the society as a social being in both high and low context cultures.

Similarity also is expressed by people when they respond to extrinsic motivations and when the motivations target basic needs, such as, food, cloths, housing, safety, socializing, esteem, and self fulfillment (O'Hair & Friedrich, 1992). Emphasizing similarity would overcome diversity. Speaking the language, performing historical moments together, sharing the pain and suffering to build the nation bond the high and low context cultures in America. Understanding the other's culture, listening effectively and promoting universal culture are factors to communicate effectively with other cultures (Harris & Moran, 1991).

In spite of people's different cultures, there are similarities. Classifications of people into high and low context cultures narrow the subject of cultural differences into stereotypes. Studying cultural differences is important because it influences an individual's communication. Culture is a broad subject which consists of people's value, rites and rituals, heroes, communication, norms, stories, and climate. Speaking the same language, performing historical moments together, and sharing the pain and suffering to build common goals bond the high and low context culture in America.

Annotated Bibliography

Harris, P. R., & Moran, R. T. (1991). <u>Managing Cultural Differences</u>.
Houston: Gulf Publishing Co. City University Library, Bellvue,
WA. September, 27-54. They argue that promoting universal culture
is a factor to communicating effectively.

Kennedy, J., & Everest, A. (1991). Put diversity in context. Personnel
Journal. September 1991. 50-53. City University Library, Bellevue
WA. They argue that people are divided into high and low context
cultures.

O'Hair, D., & Friedrich, G. W. (1992). <u>Strategic Communication in
Business and the</u>

<u>Professions</u>. Boston: Houghton Mifflin Co. 1992. City University
Bookstore, Bellevue, WA.

They argue that the components of the organization culture are values, rite and ritual, heroes, communication, norm, stories, and climate.

Hewlett, S. A. (1991). The boundaries of business: the human resource deficit. <u>Harvard Business</u>

<u>Review</u>. Jul.-Aug. 1991. 131-133, City University Library, Bellevue, WA. The author argues that the work force will consist of different cultures which will be the majority in America.

Effective Communication

Abstract

Effective communication lies on integrity and honesty for the message to be heard clearly. Communication depends on listening and probability of a message, message strategies, context, and values.

Effective Communication

"One school of thought assumes that communication between A and B has failed whenB does not accept what A has to say as being factual, true or valid and that the goal of communication is to get B to agree with A's opinion, idea, facts, or information" (Roethlisberger, 1991). "The other school of thought is quite different. It assumes that communication has failed when B does not feel free to express her/his feelings to A because B fears they will not be accepted by A" (Roethlisberger, 1991)... Both schools deal with the agreement between A and B as a problem of communication.

Feedback does not have to be a expression of acceptance. Feedback depends on the individual perception, context, coding, decoding, external noise or internal noise. Feedback could be anger, evaluation or revolution, could be smiles or tears and sadness, but only "A zero-feedback situation is said to exist when it is virtually impossible for the sender to be aware of a receiver's response" (Verdeber, 1988).

Terry's theory states that "Leadership is the activity of influencing people to strive willingly for group objectives" (O'Hair and Fredrick, 1992). This theory explains that the individual's free will shall respond to the manager's request and to accept or not to accept her/his request on her/his way of doing her/his job. Therefore, "misunderstanding may prove useful" (Clampitt, 1991) and the acceptance and agreement for un-cleared and ambiguous language and message do not reflect successful communication. The acceptance of B or her/his agreement doesn't reflect perfect communication. "Given that language is inherently ambiguous, than it is reasonable to assume that various interpretations can be assigned probabilities" (Clampitt, 1991).

In other words, A's request and B's agreement does not seem to be a boss-employee relationship. In reality the boss will say, "This is the only way to do it and I want it this way please." If the boss sees that the job should be done in certain way then s/he should command it with definite words which are direct to the point, "nevertheless, in situation that calls for specific action, directive may be more appropriate" (O'Hair & Fredrick, 1992).

The article, Barriers and Gateways to Communication by Roethlisberger assumes that the boss is logical and clear. In contrast, a boss may think s/he is logical and clear but s/he isn't. A bookkeeper was given direction not to record specific transactions and the direction was clear and logical. To be clear and logical is not always the reason for B to agree. "With any given message there are countless secondary messages that can alter the context and change the interpretations" (Clampitt, 1991). Even if A "sees himself/herself as a reasonable, logical chap," (Roethlisberger, 1991) there is no evidence B will accept A's comments or s/he would express her/his feelings to A to be accepted. A woman who responds to a clear and logical message to be there in time for a date and she was raped and murdered, shall she have effective communication because of her response to the message?

"Students are trained to be logical and clear = but no one helps them lean to listen skillfully (Roethlisberger, 1991). The bookkeeper and the woman which is mentioned above listened skillfully and they might have evaluated the message carefully but that didn't make a effective communication because the trust was shattered. Values such as, "honesty and integrity, respect for other workers, and importance of every person" (O'Hair and Fredrick, 1992) are essential for effective communication.

"Both the Bills and the Joneses of this world have good reason for opening up, especially when people believe that their true feelings or beliefs may get them fired" (Gabarro, 1991). Because the article suggests and recommends Jones' method that allows the manager to accept points of view that are different and encouraging the employee to express her/his feelings, the article failed to solve the problem of telling the truth and the consequences of telling the truth to the manager.

What if the bookkeeper who is mentioned above refused to listen to the manager and insisted to apply the Generally Accepted Accounting Principles to record all transactions. Obviously, s/he will be fired.

Evaluative listening, the context, and the awareness of certain values between A and B aare important for effective communication. If the policy of the company allows employees to criticize and express their feelings with guaranteed continuation of their job, as in Japan's manufacturing, then no problem will exist for one expressing one's feelings to her/his manager. The employee and the manager should be aware of the value behind the policy for this particular context.

Effective communication depends on a clear and logical message, context, probability of understanding the message as feedback, honesty and integrity, respect for others, and the importance of every person. Listening to clear message doesn't make the communication effective unless the message reflects honesty and integrity. Values are important factors for people to communicate effectively, also choosing the message strategy by making requests or giving directions is essential.

References

Roethlisberger, F. J. (1991). "Barriers and Gateways to Communication Part II" <u>Havard Business Review</u> (Novo/Dec. 1991): 108-111 North Point Public Library

Roethlisbeger argues that effective communication lies on skillfull listening and expressings feelings to superior.

O'hair, D. & Fredrich, G. W. (1992). "Strategic Communication in Business and the Professional" City University Bookstore. O'hair argues that values such as integrity and honesty are essential for effective communication.

Clampitt, P. G. (1991). "Communicating for Managerial Effectiveness" City University Bookstore. Clampitt argues that interpretation of message is probable.

Gabarro, J. J. (1991) "Retrospective Commentary" <u>Havard Business Review</u> (Nov./Dec. 1991) 108-109, North Point Public Library.

Gabarro argues that subordinates would probably get fired if they express their feelings to the manager.

Verderber, R. F. (1988). "Communicate" Liberty University Bookstore.

Verderber argues that effective communication lies on external or internal noise, feedback and message. The receiver will receive the correct message or incorrect message but only zero-feedback exists when it is impossible for the sender to be aware of the response.

Communication Audit

Abstract

The Maxi-Communication Audit should be developed and preserved by a code of ethics and regulations to ensure the proper use of the auditors' power as middlemen between the leaders and the subordinates. The organization should develop training programs to enhance employees' critical thinking, to encourage them to read the employee publications, and to absorb the organization's changes.

Communication Audit

The communication audit and the maxi-communication audit aren't mentioned in the text book by O'Hair and Friedrich. But the Maxi-communication Audit article by Jim Shaffer is relevant to this subject. Because it deals with issues such as the congruity of a message between the members of the organization, about what they saying, and what they are doing, and the formal communication media a channel which conveys messages between the top management and employees or vice-versa. Also the article emphasizes the issue of leadership and the appropriate way to solve the problem which involves Leader-subordinate relationships. On the other hand, it shines a light on the company's needs for people to help, facilitate, measure, counsel, and teach the leadership team to communicate effectively. The article's subject is important for communication and for the business to achieve competitive advantage and success.

The definition of internal audit "can be characterized as the connection between policy and action" (Hunn, & Meisel, 1991); in other words, the communication audit is an approach to close the gaps between the "desired condition and the actual condition (Shaffer, 1993) within the organization. The concept is fairly presented in Shaffer's article and it is logical to audit the organization messages to ensure that the messages are correctly understood. The organization may designate personnel to work as auditors but the personnel also are human beings and they can pass their favorite messages and deny the unfavorable messages.

Shaffer in his article doesn't explain how the auditors would perform their duties. Do they need code of ethics and a form of legal provision in case of intentional unethical behavior that is committed by the auditors? Auditing obviously is required for a message that is sent and received between two people or more. "These messages, when decoded, are used by people to guide individual behavior" (Shaffer, 1993). However, the organization needs auditors to ensure that the message are sent, received and implemented, to prevent what Shaffer states in his article when he says, "What employees are telling us is that while formal media (and leadership) are talking about the need for change 'My manager is doing the same old stuff he's always done" (Shaffer, 1993). According to the article, the organization should hire auditors, although they increase the company overhead.

The article states, "There's often an incongruity in what leaders say and what they do," (Shaffer, 1993) and Shaffer also suggest that the maxi-audits tell the organization to employ people who can help, facilitate, measure, counsel and teach the leader to communicate effectively. Educating the leaders is in line with the text by O'Hair and Friedrich. For example, House's Path-Goal Model in the text, elaborates on the leader's skill to "set precise goals and make the paths to these goals easier to follow" O'Hair & Friedrich, 1992). However, educating the leaders doesn't require employing people, but attending seminars and studying independently teaches leaders the meaning of leadership. Shaffer doesn't suggest the auditor should be an employee in the organization or work independently. Auditing in the accounting profession is conducted periodically and independently from the organization's management, although the management has its internal control and auditing system.

O'Hair and Friedrich state that the foundation for effective communication is the ability to think critically, and they state that the basic skill for critical thinking is reasoning, analyzing, interpreting, and evaluating. However, to enhance critical thinking skills for all employees and managers would enable them to perceive formal communication media with a better mental attitude. Instead of the employees' negative comments or their quitting reading the employee publications, they will be capable of involving in the organization's changes. In this case, the educating and encouraging critical thinking would be a effective tool and provide results greater than auditing.   "The maxi-audit assesses the communication process in its entirety. It evaluate all the ways that messages are formally and informally sent" (Shaffer, 1993)). The process of the evaluation is not understood and it is not explained in this article. Even communication-audit, as a foundation of the maxi, is not defined or explained. For example, Hunn and Meisel explain the communication process clearly, and without their definition in mind it is hard to understand the communication audit as it is explained by Shaffer. Therefore, the audit process "consists of surveying employees, observing operations, and reviewing formal and informal repots and procedures used to communicate quality information" (Hunn, & Meisel, 1991). Also, the audit process applies to "all levels of the organization (hourly, salary, management, etc.) should be audited, with the information gathered through interviews, observations, and questionnaires" (Hunn & Meisel, 1991).

If reports are considered types of messages which are exchanged in the organization, then there are no differences between maxi-communication audit and communication audit in that respect because maxi "evaluates all the ways that messages are formally and informally sent" (Shaffer, 1993) and communication audit is reviewing formal and informal reports" (Hunn & Meisel, 1991).

"Leaders who trust their co-workers are in turn, trusted by them" (Bennis, 1989). Shaffer's article doesn't tell the reader what the effect of maxi-communication audit is on the leader-subordinate relationship. The basic concept in leadership is the trust between leaders and subordinates and vice-versa. Does the maxi-communication audit create doubt or faith? Shaffer believes that the maxi-communication audit is an ultimate way for effective communication, but what about the empowerment that the auditors have. Isn't it a new power to be considered, and how far should the auditors interfere and interact between the organization's members?

Communication auditors are human beings and they are venerable to human weakness. Communication audit should be developed and preserved by a code of ethics and sort of regulations to ensure the proper use of power. The need for communication auditing is important for the organization and should be performed by independent auditors periodically and be auditors staff who are also independent from the management. On the other hand, the organization should train its employees to think critically and provide them the basic skill of reasoning, analyzing, interpreting, and evaluating. A good leader-employee relationship is based on trust, and auditing creates middlemen who have the power of controlling the content of messages. Caution nd establishing code of ethics and regulation should be considered to maintain the trust between leaders and subordinates.

Annotated Bibliography

Bennis, W. (1989). <u>On Becoming a Leader</u>. Massachusettes Mento Park: Addison- Wesley Publishing Co., City University Bookstore, Bellevue, WA. Bennis argues that leaders who trust their co-workers are in turn trusted by them.

Hunn, M.S. & Meisel, S. I. ((1991). Internal communication: auditing for quality. <u>Qualit</u>

<u>Progress</u>. June, 56-60. Dundalk Community College, Baltimore, MD. They argue that auditing can be defined as the connection between policy and action.

O'Hair, D. & Friedrich, G. W. (1992). <u>Strategic Communication in Business and</u>

profession. Boston: Houghton Mifflin Co., City University Bookstore, Bellevue, WA. They argue that the foundation for effective communication is to think critically.

Shaffer, J. (1993). The Maxi-communication audit – a precision instrument for change.

IABC Communication World. Jan. _ Feb.. 20-23. City University Library, Bellevue, WA.

Shaffer argues that the maxi-communication audit is an approach to close the gaps between the desired condition and the actual condition.

Possible New Markets

Abstract

Technology replaces human work forces which are declining naturally. However, the needs for importing labor would be decreased. Students who are the work force of the future are challenged to be superior and they have to know how to create and innovate new technology and to open possible new markets.

Possible New Markets

The article Global Work Force 2000: The new World Labor Market by William B. Johnston argues that "Nations that have slow growing work forces but rapid growth in service sector jobs (namely, Japan, Germany, and the United States) will become magnets for immigrants, even if their public policies seek to discourage them" (Johnston, 1991). But those nations are replacing workers with smart machines. The result is decreasing demands on labor. Cut off cost and layoffs are dynamic elements in competition. However, slow growing work forces are a logical progression for using technology to replace human resources.

Therefore, if a nation such as the USA with a slowly growing work force and the increasing technology which replaces human resources, the progress as a whole in America is balanced. In other words, the U.S. Market's demands on labor is declining; therefore, it matches the shortage in labor in years to come versus increases in smart machines which replace human power.

Technology which took over agricultural jobs in one of the reasons workers in America are shifting to service sector. It seems this shifting is a natural reaction to the technology that is replacing farmers with smart machines. Thus, "agricultural jobs disappear" (Johnston, 1991).

The article argues that we in America will rely on foreign labor because the market will suffer from labor shortages and the fact that high school students aren't ready for the future. "U.S. students (high school students) are performing worse relative to the rest of the world" (Johnston, 1991). In other words, it is true to say that traditional schools are not acceptable by the majority of dropout students. The U.S. market provides products which are made by the best technology in the world. Students see and realize the challenge to cooperate with traditional information versus the surrounding of the advancement of the information age. Students in the U.S.A. are challenged to be superior with a frozen educational system. American students are the work force of the future. The idea which says that the developing countries' high school graduate will supply 21% of the world's high school enrollees (Johnston, 1991) doesn't provide me with evidence that those 21% will be qualified for the American market.

"... likely many countries will make immigration easier and many workers will travel the globe" Johnston, 1991). In contrast, 'Today the same capital and labor decision is being made in factories, office and mines around the country, only today it involves substituting smart machines - the computer for other machines and labor" (Anthony, Perrewe, & Kacmar, 1993). It seems that the article is out of touch with reality in the U.S.A.. Companies in the U.S.A. "downsize" (Train, 1991) to cut costs. There are a number of factors which force American companies to downsize; such as, to attempt to lower the cost of the product, to be able to compete in the market, to attempt to earn maximum profit for its stockholders, plus the efficiency of computers and robots as a cheaper way to acquire and operate that than labor.

The strength of William B. Johnston's article is that he predicts that the increase number of older people will result in a "bigger chunk of paycheck" Johnston, 19910 that will increase the saving in America and this fund could shift to the developing countries. People have the right to travel from one country to other countries for work or fun and also people have the right to invest their money anywhere. It is human tights. The philosophy in this article is to bring to our attention that America needs its neighboros and other countries, the cooperation and trade especially with developing countries. America needs the world as much as the world needs America.

The gap between businesses and schools should be decreased. Students live in this society and realize the advanced technology surrounding them. The young people are the work force of the future and they have to know how to create and innovate new technologies and to open new markets. Technology reduces the work force which, on the other hand, is declining gradually because of the women's decision to get pregnant in older age (Johnston, 1991). Technology replaces human resources and human resources are declining naturally. Therefore, the needs for importing labor would be decreased, but America's global course of action remains prevalent.

References

Anthony, W., Perrewe, P. L., & Kacmar, K. M., (1993). <u>Strategic human resources management</u>. City University Bookstore, Bellevue, WA.

Johnston, W. B. (1991). Global work force 2000: The new world labor Market. <u>Harvard</u>

<u>Business Review</u>. (Mar.-Apr. 1991) North Point Public Library, Dundalk, MD.

Train, A. S., (1991). The case of the downsizing decision. <u>Harvard Business Review</u> Mar.-Apr. 1991). North Point Public Library, Dundalk, MD.

Network Structure

Network Structure

Did Thomson provide a positive answer to her question, "Can the Creation of Community Networks Enhance Social Capital in Rural Scotland?" The question isn't clear. Did she mean the Community Networks in general? Or did she mean the virtual networks in specific? Were her findings reliable? Did her membership in the Caithness Community change the outcome of her research? Was her research about Network Structure?

What are the reasons Laura Hamilton Thomson researched Caithness Community and in general the Community Network? Apparently, the subject is complicated and also very important to the modern world. The media, perhaps, doesn't make it any easier for people to meet and develop trust among themselves to bond in relationships. The case which Thomson presents did not emphasize the causes of the problem which led to the symptoms. Is it true the Community Networks are replacements of the newspapers? Or is it true the Community Networks are created as a result and reaction of the daily broadcasted fears through the media?

Thomson defined the social capital as "networks of trust." Trusting is an essential factor between two people, between people and society, society and government, and between people and superior powers (god and nature). If this trust is constantly shaken by the media which is broadcasting violence, criminals' news, and naturalizing the unethical philosophies then we would need desperately new avenues to express "unity, intimacy, shared morals, and freedom of expression." (Thomson, 2001).

Did Thomson achieve her goal in her study? She asked her question, "Can the creation of Community Networks enhance social capital in rural Scotland?" and did she deliver the answers? The Quantitative Data Analysis helped to draw a picture of the community in action. Figure 4.1 includes the nationality as independent variables and the frequency of the visits by the member of the community of different nationalities to the Caithness website as dependent variables. There is a natural zero which indicates the ratio level of measurement is used in the graph of Figure 4.1. The nature zero in this graph indicates the complete absent of the members' visits to the Caithness website.

On the other hand, Figure 4.1 indicates that there is no way to measure the difference between one attribute and another. The attributes, in Figure 4.1, are the nationalities of the members of the community. In spite of the natural zero, the graph fits the ordinal level of measurement.

Figure 4.2 indicates that there is no arbitrary or natural zero but there is order of rank or class of some sort; however, the graph of Figure 4.2 indicates ordinal level of measurement because a member of the community can be included in a category 45-65 of age but we actually do not know the magnitude of the differences between the categories. The graph helps the readers to realize the different ages of the population and their different interests. The significance of this pie graph is to target those segments of the population who are not participating in this type of technology. Thomson doesn't elaborate on the reasons why certain segments of the population do not utilize this technology.

Figure 4.3 includes independent variables (everyday, weekly, and monthly) and dependent variables which indicate the frequency of visits of the members of the community to the website. The bar graph of Figure 4.3 is the reflection of the interval level of measurement because the data begin with an arbitrary zero. If the data begin with a natural zero the researcher would utilize the ratio level of measurement. The significance of this graph is to show that the community is offering information which the members find interesting (Thomson, 2001). But because the research sample (82 members) is relatively small perhaps the data might be misleading!

In addition, in Figure 4.3, because the arbitrary zero is the beginning of data and it is possible to measure the difference between one attribute and another (days, weeks, and months) the graph fits the interval level of management. It is an arbitrary zero because the month breaks down to weeks ... days ... hours ... minutes ... seconds ...and infinite smaller units than the second.

Thomson was very clever to join Caithness Community to investigate the Community Network. But there is downside for being a member of a group. When the group members know a member is researching the community the behavior might not be as natural as it should be. The attention which Thomson is giving to the group would change the behavior of the group, perhaps, positively or negatively.

Joining an organization to do research about the organization is not practical. If I want to research AT&T it might not be possible to join the work force at AT&T. In this case, Thomson was able to be a member of the community but perhaps it is not the usual way to conduct a research if the researcher is an independent or student. As a student I would imagine my research would be about small businesses because I spent long years and hours working for small businesses and I am still working for small businesses.

Caithness Community reminds me of the MSN Communities Networks. There are similarities and also critical differences. Caithness Community is a closed community in which the member has to have a password and login name. The MSN Community is controlled by the manager who might allow access of the members to different features. Thomson described the main features as asynchronous and synchronous means of communications.

Thomson succeeded to inform the Internet surfers about the Caithness Community. Although, it is very interesting case, at least now I know about Caithness Community and town as a case study, but honestly without my enrollment in this course perhaps I would never hear of this town or site. What are the chances for the people around the globe to read about a small rural town? Thomson, definitely, was aware that Caithness Community is well known by the people of Caithness town. Caithness Community Network is an example of a healthy small community and a whole world to its members.

Thomson and others discuss the decline in the social networks. (Thomson). Whatever the reason is, fear or a life style that is a result of the technological impact on the world, the truth is that the society should develop new avenues to communicate. Has Caithness Community reached the social capital as defined by Thomson? There are signs for the positive result from creating the Caithness Community Network.

In spite of the virtual reality, the members are frequently visiting the site for recreation, local information, and the community activities. (Thomson). These visitations are positive social behavior but the question is, does the frequency of visits to the site have anything to do with the networks of trust? Perhaps visiting the site frequently is the sign of negative activities!! Thomson's findings are based on her reputation as a researcher among the community members. The members of the community were getting attention from Thomson; however, the result of her research and her findings might not be accurate. Special attention might change the output, "output went up regardless of changes, a result attributed to special attention paid to the people." (Weisboro, 1987, p. 93).

The presentation and the formatting of the dissertation of Thomson do not follow exactly the American Psychological Association (APA) documentation style. Thomson's quotations are in blocks, larger font size, and bold. It is an innovative way to present her work. The way she arranged the quotations undermined her personal opinion, interpretation of the data, and findings. The readers, especially the members of Caithness Community, perhaps were interested to read about her findings in bold letters. She departed from the APA documentation style already so if she were focusing the formatting on her opinion, interpretation of the data, and findings the presentation probably will be more effective.

Her quotations from the members of the community are in bold and a larger size font to indicate her concern about the members' opinions and contributions to her research. Manipulating the members in a positive way is a delicate subject and she was aware of it. It was an implied statement of her gratitude from her to the members of the community to allow her to be a part of the community and to be her vehicle for her research objectives.

In general, Thomson's published paper is an effective tool to advertise for Caithness Community. It seems that the research of this community by Thomson contributes to the popularity of Caithness Community. Perhaps her contribution will encourage the director of this community, Bill Ferni, to consider imposing membership fees.

Thomson probably should have used descriptive statistics to make her presentation more useful. Using Mode, for example, to inquire how many people in this population are willing to pay an equal amount of a suggested membership fee, and agreed by the majority, would be a great help to the director of the community. Using Mean, also, would determine how much members of the community will accept lower or higher than the middle of the suggested membership fee. Or by using Median, the director will be able to average the price and expect a positive outcome.

Thomson had not solved the financial problem which Caithness will face sooner or later. The Interview Questions were not enough to generate discussion or to provide introduction to what will happen if the community doesn't contribute financially to maintain the Caithness Community on the Internet. Thomson's paper doesn't have useful recommendations to help this community to survive the next 5 or 10 years. There is no sense for researching and collecting data without recommending solutions to the problem which the organization is facing.

Thomson collected data. The quantitative and qualitative techniques which were provided by Thomson stated facts. Thomson lacked the vision to the future. She didn't answer the question of how this community is going from point A to point B and beyond. She stated the need for financial support but she didn't investigate, statistically, the possibilities for a successful financial solution.

Finally, did Thomson answer her question "Can the Creation of Community Networks Enhance Social Capital in Rural Scotland?" When I read her definition of "social capital," I was expecting data about unity, intimacy, shared morals, and freedom of expression, but I found instead the quantitative and qualitative techniques were used completely for the structure of Caithness Community Network. Although, her membership was a clever idea to collect information about Caithness Network, her data probably were misleading because members may have acted differently as soon as they knew they were being given extra attention.

References

Thomson, L.H. (2001). *Can the Creation off Community Networks Enhance Social Capital in Rural Scotland?* Retrieved December 14, 2002, from TUI University Website.

(1987). *Productive workplaces organizing and managing for dignity, meaning, and community p. 93.* San Francisco: Jossey-Basss.

The Physical Impact: Is It Science or Fiction?

The Physical Impact: Is It Science or Fiction?

Physical Strength and Job Performance is a case study and the subject of this paper. The case is created by the Rice Virtual Lab in Statistics. The primary analyses indicate that the case under scrutiny has two sides. The first side is the ethical and legal consequences; and the second side is the measurements of physical ability and the relationships between variables. The following pages are limited to the analyses of the measurement of physical strength and the relationship between variables. The question is: Is the physical testing of the prospective employees based on scientific experiments? If the employee is not fit for the job physically, what are the reasonable tests that were performed to conclude the disqualifications?

The variables in this case are the grip strength, arm strength, supervisor ratings, simulation scores, the work performed and the test information. Among other ideas, this paper is to examine the following idea "Measures of strength of association should not be thought of as something that proves causation, but only as a measure of covariation in the measurements" (Eveland, 2003). The idea perhaps is true because the test information in itself as an independent variable doesn't cause the arm to be strong or weak. The time, two seconds, of testing the arm strength doesn't mean the test contributes to the strength of the arm but it only measures the strength.

But maybe there is an exception to the previous rule because directly or indirectly one characteristic may be caused by variation of the other. For example, if the employee was not properly informed of critical details of the test and how to use the equipment the result of the arm strength probably will not indicate the correct readings. Another example, in a work simulation, the work might not be suitable for the prospective performer and the supervisor ratings accordingly will indicate a wrong score. The cause and effect in both examples are detected because of the direct causality of the independent variables on the dependent variables.

Co-variation of the two variables, grip strength and arm strength, probably due to a common cause which is the muscle size or physical fitness of the prospective employee. The size of the muscle and the physical fitness of the individual are causes that might affect both the grip strength and the arm strength equally. In contrast, the causes which are affecting two variables might not necessarily affect both variables in the same ways. For example, the supervisor ratings, perhaps, are influenced by outside disturbances, fatigue e.g., during the late hours in the day.

The causal relationship between the supervisor ratings and arm strength may be a result of inter-dependent relationships. For example, other variables; such as, resting between tasks probably has an effect on both the supervisor ratings and arm strength. If the prospective employee is not getting the proper resting his/her performance will be less or poor and the supervisor ratings accordingly will be lower because the performance of the prospective employee doesn't meet the standard.

If a researcher is working on a project to set the standard for work procedures and timing each task, the researcher has to choose randomly selected individuals who are experienced in the field. The researcher might choose sampling intervals to collect his/her sample. From a list which contains the names of those individuals the researcher might choose the odd numbers, even numbers, or choose five, or another number, as an equal interval. Here the association of the sample versus population is due to chance alone (Torchim, 2000)

Extreme values in a variable, outliers, might affect the test outcomes and the strength of the association. If the collected data includes extreme values, extremely high or low, the researcher probably will have a mean which in itself is a higher average than the one that excludes the extreme values. The confidence interval and the statistical significance will have different readings.

It is not imaginable that the grip strength and the arm strength are not related variables in this case. Physically speaking, both variables are a result of autocorrelation. The result of Jackson Evaluation System which is designed to test the grip strength is not designed to calculate the nerve strength in the arm that is a part of the overall nervous system.

If the correlation between a particular test and a measure of subsequent job performance is .2 then .2 indicates that the prediction of one measurement from the other measurement is closer to the zero which indicates the absence of the linear relation and correlation coefficients. The correlation coefficient should be between −1 and +1, that is, +1 implies complete similarities and −1 implies dissimilarities. However, the square of .2 is 4% which indicates the ability to predict one measure from the other by only 4%. On the other hand, the square of .8 which is 64% implies the ability to predict one measure from the other by 64%. (Fitzgerald, 2001).

The correlation between the test and a measure of subsequent job performance would be acceptable as valid personnel screening mechanism if the correlation were .8 (64%) because the ability to predict the other measurement is closer to +1 the complete similarities. On the other hand, .2 (4%) indicates less ability to predict the other measurement.

The relationship between the variables in the sample versus the variable relationships in the population is calculated as p-value. The probability p value is actually 5% and if the percentage is less than 5% the relationship between the variables in the sample should be a good indicator as representative of the relation between variables in the population. The 5% is actually the error or the fluke in the sample. The p value is calculated by the T-Test. In other words, if p is less than 5% then the relation between the variables in the sample is significant. For example, the supervisor ratings and the standardized work simulations should conclude similar results. A statistically significant relationship between a measure of physical capability and a measure of job performance is less than practically significant if p-value is higher than 5%.

In some instances, a variable A causes the occurrence of another variable B. For example, height of an individual is associated with a heavier body weight of that individual. The taller the person is the heavier the weight. Another example, the more food, quantity, the individual eats as a result of depression or other obesity disorders the fatter the individual will be. A positive relationship between two variables would appear clearly if line graph is used. Also job performance, in this case, is driven from testing the strength of the prospective employees who applied for the job and hired. Linear regression is a great statistical tool to predict the performance of workers in the future.

Testing can meaningfully predict job performance and reduce and prevent injuries on the job. Although, this case is about physical testing the mental testing is still at large. Learning on the job and training a person to perform certain tasks should be taken into consideration when an employer is faced by the hiring dilemma. Is the physical testing science or fiction? Of course, the testing of the physical strength is science, but is it comprehensive and indicative of human potential? The answer is No!! The injuries and accidents are probably the result of the mental state of the individual at the moment of the accident or injury!

References

Coe, R. (2000). *What is an effect size?* Retrieved January 25, 2003, from website: http://cem.dur.ac.uk/ebeuk/research/effectsize/ESguide. htm

Eveland, J.D. (2003). *Eveland's disquisition on data analysis.* Retrieved January 25, 2003, from website: http://graduate.tourou.edu/ bus600d3/Modules/module04/disquisition.htm

FitzGerald, J. (2001) *Decisionmaking index (previous feature articles).* Retrieved January 25, 2003, from: http://www.coolth.com/ index2.htm

Lowery, R. (1999). *A first glance at the question of statistical significance.* Retrieved January 25, 2003, from website: http://graduate. tourou.edu/bus600d3/modules/module04/Ch4%20Intro%20 Statistical% 20Significance.htm

Med-Tox Health Services (2003). *Strength test validation for employee selection*. Retrieved January 25, 2003, from http://home.earthlink. net/~medtox/test.html

Rice Virtual Lab in Statistics (2000). *Physical strength and job performance*. Retrieved January 25, 2003, from Website: http://www.ruf. rice.edu/~lane/case_studies/physical_strength/index.html

Trochim, W. M. (2000). *Sampling*. Retrieved January 25, 2003, from:

http://faculty.ncwc.edu/toconnor/308/308lect03.htm Virginia Tech. (1999). *Statistical and models in the social sciences*. Retrieved January 25, 2003,   from: http://pse.cs.vt.edu/SoSci/converted/

The Mystery of the Gentleman Variable

The Mystery of the Gentleman Variable

Two studies are the subjects of this case study. The first study is *An Empirical Study of the Causal Antecedents of Customer Confidence in E-Tailers* by Sandeep Krishnamurthy and the other study is *Organizational Commitment and ethical Behavior: An Empirical Study of Information System Professionals* by Effy Oz. The first study is concerned with the level of confidence and to develop effective e-tailer's website. The second study is concerned with the organizational commitment and ethical behavior of the Information System professionals.

The narrative of this case will be combined into general ideas and the remaining part is the analyses for both studies. The general ideas are about the introductions and the problem statements or research questions and the general concepts. The next section is the comparison and contrast of the two studies. And the remaining part is about the statistical issues and the construction and effective research tools and hypotheses used in both studies.

The first observation is that the first study, E-Tailers article, is interesting but it leans toward incomplete information. The reason apparently is to avoid the inconsistency in the study presentation. For example, is it true that the seal of approval is helping the customer to trust the e-tailer or it is a new costly burden to the e-tailer? To obtain, for example, the seal of approval from the Better Business Bureau the company has to be a member who has to pay a monthly fee (Krishnamurthy, 2001).

The second question is that: is it true the company who is advertising heavily stands behind its product and that what the consumers believe? Take eBay as an example, eBay company is surviving mostly on the fees collected from each member seller. The problem with eBay is that the seller who failed to sell his/her product will terminate his/her membership and will never return to eBay as a seller or even as a buyer. It is a dilemma for eBay. This dilemma, perhaps, is the number one cause behind its advertisement (2001).

The same concept should be applied to McDonald Corporation. Although McDonald is not e-tailer the advertising techniques are similar for both the on-ground and the online businesses. The unhealthy food is the product of McDonald and the heavy advertising is the effect of the constant reminder of their unhealthy food. Will McDonald offer reduced calories food? High calories are related to an obesity epidemic in America as a result of the food that McDonald offers to the public.

What is the percentage of death which is associated with high calorie diets?

On the other hand, the broken links probably are a good reason for the customers to shy away from the website. The E-Tailers article states that the broken links or the incorrect grammar used and included on the website are both contributing to the customer low confidence in the e-tailer. It is a good observation by Krishnamurthy (2001).

In general, probably the navigational difficulty is a common reason for the e-tailer customers in which they encounter during each time they try to buy anything from the e-tailers. For example, Amazon.com has many alternatives when choosing a book, by the title, the author name, or keyword. The books are classified by the lowest price, highest price, the best selling, or featured books.

Although, these features in Amazon.com are great features they are limited in the small e-tailer. For example, 1stbooks.com has only limited features. 1stbooks.com doesn't allow the customer to navigate first the end or the middle of the list of the books but this feature that allow its customers to navigate first the end or the middle of the list of the books is seen at Barnes and Noble. The customers have the choice.

In the second study, the IS article, the introduction is relatively shorter than the first study. Effy Oz, the author of the second study, refers to the failure of the information system (IS) professionals to their unethical behavior. Oz doesn't ask questions. Oz claims that the unethical behavior is the reason for the failure of the IS professionals. It is a strong statement but there is no way to guess the variables in this particular claim Oz is proposing (Oz, 2001).

By comparison, Krishnamurthy successfully makes the introduction interesting; in contrast, Oz lacks the excitement in the introduction. Krishnamurthy includes declarative sentences and prepares the reader to interesting findings. Krishnamurthy uses statements to illustrate the variables in each problem. For example, Krishnamurthy related the broken links, in a website, by delivering the products to customers. The broken links are independent variables (attribute) and delivering the products is the dependent variable.

The principle variables included in the E-Tailer article are:

Independent Variable (IV) – broken links

Dependent Variable (DV) – confidence level

Negative relationship

IV – correct grammar

DV – increase confidence level

Positive relationship

IV – confidence

DV – increase gross sales

Positive relationship:

IV – warranties

DV – increase gross sales

Positive relationship

DV – product commitment

IV – increase advertising expenditure

Positive relationship

The principle variables included in the IS professional article are:

IV – ethical behavior

DV – decrease turnover rate

Negative relationship:

IV – corporate ethical values

DV – increase or decrease organizational commitment

Positive or negative relationship

IV – congruence of corporate and employee's value

DV – increase organizational commitment

Positive relationship

IV– congruence

DV – decrease employees' turnover

Negative relationship

There are many variables that should be examined. For example, the specific information of a product is important for the general public; however, if a collector is collecting videos of a French actor or actress the video site should state if the movie is subtitled or not. The variables are:

IV – add specific information to the site

DV – increase gross sale and decrease the number of angry buyers

The second sets of variables are: why should an Internet buyer buys from this website? Is the payment method, usually credit card, secured? Does the website's owner or staff act professionally? The casual email turns the buyer away from the website. The formal, mass reproduced, and impersonal email to confirm receiving the order or shipping the product enhances customer satisfaction. And the most important variable is the word of mouth and reputation among the population.

On the other hand, ethics and the relationships which are generated due to the market need for the IS professionals vary from one individual to another. The competence and ethics probably are related variables. Lack of advanced technical education and the severity of the technical problems are related variables which affect the IS ethical behavior. The customers' poor technical knowledge of the technical problem at hand is another factor for increasing the lawsuits among the IS professionals who are appointed to solve the problem.

When adding specific information to the site, independent variable, and decrease the number of angry buyers, dependent variable, are used to formulate a hypothesis the declarative sentence would be: this study is to determine the relationship between the information level provided on the site and the number of the unsatisfied buyers. This hypothesis is reasonable because the e-tailers are concerned mainly about the profit.

They rely on vague information they provide for any product, a French movie e.g., to increase the sale (Torchim, 2002).

When the buyer who bought the French movie discovers there is no translation from the French language to English s/he will be disappointed and will return the movie to the e-tailer. Time was spent to look for the movie on the Internet, shipping cost was expensed by the e-tailer, and cost was expensed to ship back the product, plus the paperwork and the inventory tracking are also were expenses which could be prevented if the word "subtitled" was on the site of the movie.

The subtitled word is an example of the specific information which should be added to the product. The hypothesis is interesting because the e-tailers assume the customer has previous information about the product. In many cases, the customer is looking for something interesting on the Internet and s/he is willing to buy what s/he sees. Collectors are looking for the last century's products and the motion picture is an important part of the human culture and actually it is a huge reflection of the time which the motion picture was produced.

The declarative statement is: the customers' poor technical knowledge of the technical problem at hand is another factor for increasing the unethical behavior and the lawsuits among the IS professionals who are appointed to solve the problem. The hypothesis would be: this study is to determine the relationship between the level of education and the number of the malpractice lawsuits (2002).

The hypothesis is reasonable because the consequences of the unethical behavior will lead eventually to a lawsuit. The difficulty to determine how many lawsuits are based on unethical behavior is definitely a challenge and a problem that should be addressed. The study of the lawsuits probably leads to other hypotheses.

The IS professional article is based on the a study of differences because the hypotheses use ethics as a preexisting variable unlike the E-Tailers article costumers' confidence is post-existing variable and as study of associations.

In conclusion, The E-Tailers article is well grounded in both theory and practice. The hypotheses are clear and serve the purpose from the study. Perhaps, more detail would make the IS professionals article interesting. The negative relationship of the variable was worthy of note. Both articles include new ideas and add new perspective to the researchers who studied them and probably enjoyed them.

References

Dereshiwsky, M. (1998). *Introduction to research: it starts with a question.* Retrieved January 11, 2003, from Website: http://trochim.human. cornell.edu/kb/contents.htm

Dereshiwsky, M. (1998). *Introduction to research: Understanding variable.* Retrieved January 11, 2003, from Website: http://jan.ucc.nau. edu/~mid/edr610/class/variables/variables/lesson3-1-1.html

Dereshiwsky, M. (1998). *Introduction to research: Understanding hypotheses.* Retrieved January 11, 2003, from Website: http://jan. ucc.nau.edu/~mid/edr610/class/variables/hypotheses/lesson3-2-1. html

Krishnamurthy, S. (2001). *An empirical study of the causal antecedents of customer confidence in e-tailers.* Retrieved January 11, 2003,website: http://www.firstmonday.dk/issues/issue6_1/krishnamurthy/#k3

Oz, E. (2001). *Organizational commitment and ethical behavior: an empirical study of information system professionals.* Retrieved January 11, 2003, website: http://graduate.tourou.edu/bus600d3/Modules/module03/Organizational%20commitme nt.htm.

Marion, R., (2001). *The whole art of deduction: research skills for new scientists.* Retrieved January 11, 2003, from Website: http://trochim.human.cornell.edu/kb/contents.htm

The National Health Museum. *Formatting Hypotheses.* Retrieved January 11, 2003, from Website: http://www.accessexcellence.com/21st/TL/filson/formathypo.html

Torchim, W. M., (2002). *Research methods knowledge base.* Retrieved January 11, 2003, from http://trochim.human.cornell.edu/kb/contents.htm

The Design

The Design

The subject of this paper is about an article called "Integrating workspace design, web-based tools and organizational behavior" which is authored by Joe Mort and John Knapp of the Xerox Wilson Center for Research and Technology. Mort and Knapp conducted an experiment. The article claimed to answer "complex questions" which were not stated or mentioned in forms of questions. The article also claimed the experiment includes four change agents: workspace design, budget, organization, and technology.

The article analyzed three of the change agents but neglected "budget" as a change agent. The other three change agents were mentioned and analyzed. The independent variables were manipulated and the experiment was a continued experiment that lasted for one year. The design of a series research is based on a sequence of events and observations. The LX experiment is qualified as a qualitative research experiment, "pursued within the LX Competency Laboratory of the Xerox Corporation's Wilson Center for Research & Technology (WCR&T)."

Is this study an "experiment" which studies a situation before and after treatment? The LX experiment began with staff and management members, workspace, technology, and the interventionists. There were no statistical and numerical measurements to evaluate the performance of the staff. There is no correlation coefficient between variables. There is no clear association between the independent variables and the dependent variables. The experiment is a study of qualitative data.

The characteristics of this experimental design are the manipulation of the change agents, and the observations. The control of the experiment was not strong or defined and the unacceptable behavior in normal circumstances was treated as innovation. For example, when a member of the group leaves the conference because the subject of the meeting is not interesting the remaining members might feel the same way or at least will be disturbed by the departure of those members; however, is that innovation or disturbance?

The experiment should be controlled. The data which were collected were dealing with the qualitative dependent variables. The observation as a measurement doesn't reflect the reality most of the time. What one person interprets as a positive behavior perhaps the same behavior would be interpreted by another person as a negative behavior! The LX experiment did not have numerical data to measure the outcomes.

The true experimental design is based on causality or cause and effect and/or the correlation between variables and random assignment is used (Trochim, 2002). The LX experiment was controlled and the cause and effect between the independent variable and the dependent variables were not clear. The workspace, technology, and organization are considered independent variables and people, mission, and work culture are dependent variables. The change in the independent variables causes changes in behavior and work culture and the organization's memory but there was no before treatment and after treatment (Smith, 1997).

Actually, there was no explanation for why participants behaved the way they did in the LX Commons. Was the behavior in the LX Commons a result of the workspace arrangement or as a result of lack of concentration? The researchers compromised the need to work individually and privately for a period of time. The LX Commons dominated the experiment as a place lacking organization. Was LX experimental design a true experimental design? Probably it was a quasi-experimental design because there was no definite evidence to support the answer of the research questions.

The compromises were reflected in the lack of the organization and the increase of disturbance. The compromises were necessary as a part of the experiment design. If the LX Commons was in an isolated area such as a conference room the technology, PCs e.g., should be in another area. The design would be no different than the classical design in a traditional organization.

The inferences made from this research are sort of coerced and artificial inferences. The design of the LX Commons was the heart of the experiment. The LX Commons was used as a conference room and the PCs were used for research and development. The participants had to use the computers for research in the LX Commons during a conference and while the other participants were wandering around for unrelated activities. The LX Commons looks like a chaotic place.

The balance of quantitative and qualitative data elements in this study doesn't exist!! The variables which are used in this experiment are mostly based on qualitative data. For example, the workspace, electronic tools, LX knowledge base, adaptability, and coherent mission are all qualitative data. There were no numerical data and accordingly there were no statistical methods and techniques used. Employee Motivation/ Satisfaction Survey (EMS) was used and probably the information generated from the survey should be used to generate statistical output. The experiment did not mention the survey was used to generate statistical outcomes (Foley, 2003).

The kinds of data, of which they probably ought to have had more, are the quantitative data. For example, the knowledge bank should be manipulated to study how many participants log-in in a day, and how long they stay logging in. What type of subject in which they are interested? The knowledge bank should be monitored and controlled by the administrator using a specific password for tracking each participant. Data are collected by the administrator should be analyzed statistically to allocate the cost of the research based on the outcomes.

The kinds of data, of which they probably ought to have had less, are data which are collected from the workspace and LX Commons as a common place for a chaotic interaction among the participants. Systemizing the chaos is unusual in the work place. Brainstorming might lead to innovations and inventions but it should be done within a group of people who share a common interest unlike the LX Commons as a common place which lacks a common interest among the participants!!

The most useful aspects of the design of the LX experiment were the concentration on the qualitative data. No doubt the experiment was successful as a design of an organizational structure. It probably is a new idea to systemize the lack of organization and to use qualitative data and observations. On the other hand, the least useful aspects of the design of the LX experiment is the experiment itself. The outcomes of the experiment are based on probability; for example, adaptability is not a sign of healthy environment or a good design. A human being is adaptive by nature to any circumstances.

The critical mistake which the researchers made was the statement they said and they didn't prove. The article said, "This article provides an account of the practical steps taken and some assessment of the progress made toward identifying new work and organizational practices that can provide tangible and measurable improvements in the internal business added-value of R&D" (Mort and Knapp, 1999). The researchers claimed that they are going to provide "tangible and measurable improvements" which was a false claim because their findings were not measured and the outcomes were true probability, as in quasi-experimental design, not definite or measured.

In general, the findings reported by the researchers are questionable. But the question is: Can researchers use only observations as a means to measure the variables in an experiment? Inductive research is a way to research beginning with observations and ending with a theory. However, the research should not jump from observations to a theory without conducting tests to measure the variables correlation, association, significance, and regression. Although, the qualitative data in a research is acceptable the quantitative data would help the researcher to gain control over the sample and to decide if the sample represents, in fact, the population.

The area of activity, the domain, which the researchers should extend their findings, is LX Commons. The reason for the need for a further study for the LX Commons is that it is a place where the creativity is conceived and the communications are complicated and wrapped in uncertainty. Although, the researchers did not extend their findings for

LX Commons as a major activity area the researchers' effort, in this area of activity, was noticeable.

Based on readings in research design, there are two non-experimental quantitative researches as alternatives which the researcher can use as research designs. These designs would also be helpful in answering the research questions involved in this study. The two non-experimental research designs are causal-comparative research and correlational research. The causal-comparative design involves the cause and effect among relationships. In contrast the correlational research design involves the relationship among variables and the ability to make predictions (Burke, 2000).

Although, the article explained the LX experiment in detail, the experiment provided findings that were not enough to explain all the elements and the relationships among variables. The initial statement by the researchers "The improvements sought can be in the number of technology options produced by an R&D organization, their quality (as measured by perceived business value) and the speed or efficiency with which they are generated." was researched but the technology options were limited. The experiment was done by qualitative data and there were no quantitative data available to test the outcomes.

References

Foley, D. (2003). *Quantitative research vs. qualitative research.* Retrieved February 8, 2003, from website: http://www.windsor.igs. net/~nhodgins/quant_qual.html#SOURCES

Heaton, J. (1998). *Secondary of qualitative data.* Retrieved February 8, 2003, from website: http://graduate.tourou.edu/bus600d3/ Modules/module05/background%20Materials/So c i a l % 2 0 Research%20Update%2022%20Secondary%20analysis%20 of%20qualitative%2   0data.htm

Johnson, B. (2000). *Toward a new classification of nonexperimental quantitative reseach.* Retrieved February 8, 2003, website: http://graduate.tourou.edu/bus600D3/modules/ module05/research%20question/aera3   00202.pdf

Mort, J. and Knapp, J. (1999). *Integrating workspace design, web-based tools and* *organizational behavior.* Retrieved February 8, 2003, website: http://graduate.tourou.edu/bus600d3/modules/module05/Integrating%20workspace%2 0design.htm

Smith, L. (1997). *Research design.* Retrieved February 8, 2003,from: http://www.hlth.curtin.edu.au/psych/units/04686/design.htm

Trochim, W. (2002*). Types of designs.* Retrieved February 8, 2003, from: http://trochim.human.cornell.edu/kb/destypes.htm

Zarhan, E. (2003). *A comment on causal inference based on correlational event-related fMRI results.* Retrieved February 8, 2003, from website: http://graduate.tourou.edu/bus600D3/modules/module05/research%20question/correlati on_commentary.pdf

Which Side of the Brain?

Which Side of the Brain?

This paper is about a research report titled: *Does the Gun Pull the Trigger? Automatic Priming Effects of Weapon Pictures and Weapon Names* By Craig A. Anderson, Arlin J. Benjamin, JR., and Bruce D. Bartholow of the University of Missouri–Columbia. The article is the extension study of Berkowitz and LePage (1967). The question of the research is expressed in the title of the research. Is the research question questionable? This paper discusses the issues and the alternatives to add other perspectives.

The presence of a weapon doesn't necessarily trigger aggressive behavior but the mental imagery. The presence of a man in a hand fighting doesn't mean the arms were a prime to aggressive behavior!! A presence of a woman in a rape case doesn't mean her beauty was a prime to aggressive behavior!! The presence of a weapon doesn't necessarily mean every murderer in America committed her/his crime because s/

he had a weapon in her/his possession and this weapon triggered the aggressive behavior.

Craig Anderson, et al, in their research did not prove facts about the relationships between physical weapons and aggressive behavior. The idea of the experiment was deeper than its procedures and findings. The weapons/aggressive behavior relationships were based on the words the researchers used with participants. The words are not physical weapons neither the picture of weapons. Words or pictures are mental images. The experiment proves that the mental images of weapons can trigger aggressive behavior not necessarily the physical weapons.

If a man wants to kill another man and he doesn't have a weapon his imagination will dictate his choice of the type of weapon which he will need to use for killing that man. Anderson in his research report, *Does the gun pull the trigger?* tries to prove that the photo of a gun triggers aggressive behavior; ironically, he contradicted himself in his article "Examining an affective aggression framework: weapon and temperature effects on aggressive thoughts, affect, and attitude." Anderson said is this article that "We therefore expected that gun photos would not influence feeling of hostility" (Anderson, Anderson, and Deuser, 1996, p 369).

By evaluating the science that underlies this debate in this experiment probably the science is effective only if the researcher gathered all facts. The experiment was conducted on students between 18 and 24 of age. The research claimed that the experiment is about reading skills. Were the students reacting to the claim? There is a doubt that the result of the experiment was clear cut about aggression or about demonstrating the reading skill.

It seems that the balance between science and ideology in the articles and other similar materials is unbalanced. The idea is that if the researcher intends to research weapons and aggression perhaps the prisons would be the first choice. The court records also will be a good choice to start a research about weapons and aggression. The ideology behind the research report is interesting and for the gun control issue in the present time. The science to conduct the experiment was not convincing.

The Anderson et al. article is a lab experiment design. The first advantage of the lab experiment is the high control level. The second advantage is that the students are randomly selected. The third advantage is the well defined intervention. The forth advantage is that definitiveness of conclusion. The forth advantage perhaps is not precisely an advantage in this research report, the subject of this paper. The disadvantage of this experiment is the artificial environment, the misleading purpose of the experiment, and the fictional illustration and reasons of the experiment. What are some of the advantages and disadvantages of this kind of design in approaching this sort of issue? (Williams, 2003)

The alternative designs that might also get at learning about this issue are a) a field experiment, and b) a correlational/associational study. The field experiment is probably fits this type of research. The interviewing of the prisoners, for example, about their crimes would result in a factual conclusion. On the other hand, the correlational statistical study also using the prisoners themselves will result in very important data. These statistical data would predict the future and how to prevent the person to be victimized or to be aggressive in the difficult situations.

The basic research question is badly framed because this research has flaws which are the use of participants who are misled by the fictional objectives and reasons. The research focused on the wrong parts of human behavior because the reasons for the experiment, claimed by the researcher, were to conduct reading skills and probably the students were using the part in the brain that is responsible for the reading skills. The research question which will be fit for the scientific research is: Does the DNA have anything to do with the aggressive behavior. And why do people behave differently toward weapons?

The other aspects of this research problem that seem significant are the association of weapons with the freedom of the people. What if a country, whose people are disarmed, is controlled by a dictator? The military is not the issue here but the innocent civilian people in a country. Another research question would be what will people do if a dictator controlled the military and the voting power was lost forever? Freedom is taken for granted in America and many other countries. The gun control probably is a good idea but vaguely prevent people from killing each other. How about knives and baseball bats? They are also weapons in the hands of criminals and, if proven, people with a defective DNA.

Another aspect of this research is the alcohol and illegal drugs and the aggressive behavior. What is the effect of these substances on an armed person? What are the relationships between these substances, weapons, and aggressive behavior? What are the relationships between uneducated persons and these substances? Are the uneducated individuals receptive to these substances and the aggressive behavior? Does the social or the economic situation increase or decrease the aggressive behavior and the possession of guns?

In conclusion, to say the gun pulls the trigger is not precisely accurate. The research, by Anderson, et al, is based on a lie. This lie complicated the research and the results were in valid. The participants thought that the experiment was about reading skill; however, they used the part in the brain for reading skills. If participants were told the truth the brain perhaps would react differently. The participants did not have fear factors or self defense environments to react appropriately. The participants of this research should be people who previously used the gun to harm someone. The correlational research would be appropriate for this research to use the statistical outcomes for understanding and predicting the future. The scientific question should be asked and the study should be comprehensive.

References

Anderson, C., Benjamin A., & Bartholow B. (1998). *Does The Gun Pull The Trigger?* Retrieved March 23, 2003, from Website: http://www.psychology.iastate.edu/faculty/caa/abstracts/Aggression/Media.html

Anderson C. Anderson D. & Deuser W. (1996). *Examining An Affective Aggression Framework: Weapon and Temperature Effects on Aggressive Thoughts, Affect, and Attitude.* Retrieved March 23, 2003, from Website: http://www.psychology.iastate.edu/faculty/caa/abstracts/Aggression/Media.html

Anderson, C & Bushman, B. (2001). *Effects of Violent Video Games on Aggressive Behavior, Aggressive Cognition, Aggressive Affect, Physiological Arousal, and Prosocial Behavior: A Meta-Analytic Review of the Scientific Literature.* Retrieved March 23, 2003, from

Website: http://www.psychology.iastate.edu/faculty/caa/abstracts/ Aggression/Media.html

Johnson, B. (2000). *Toward a New Classification of Nonexperimental Quantitative Research.* Retrieved March 23, 2003, from Website: http://graduate.tourou.edu/bus601m3/modules/module01/ background.htm

Williams, E. (2003). *Experimental Methods.* Retrieved March 23, 2003, from Website: http://graduate.tourou.edu/bus601m3/modules/ module01/experimental_methods.htm

Internet Society

Internet Society

Internet and Society: a preliminary Report by Norman H. Nie and Lutz Erbring of Stanford Institute for the Quantitative Study of Society is concerned about the Internet and the Society as separate entities. The social change affected by the Internet is the theoretical construct of the study. Probably the operational definitions of the study are summarized in many questions such as: Who are the users of the Internet? What are the consequences of using the Internet? How did the Internet affect the behavior of the users?

The study converted the operational definition questions into measurable variables; such as, age of the users, hours spent on the Internet, gender, retirement, and Internet years. The study of Nie and Erbring was conducted on the Internet. Of course, the study was an exclusive study which doesn't include non-Internet users. The study did not mention the effect of growing educational institutions that are using the Internet as necessity. The researchers study the Internet as a replacement of the television and an alternative of an entertainment industry, but they didn't study the Internet as a necessary military or educational evolution in our time.

The interesting part of the study is that the researchers did not talk about the shifting of the traditional university to the Internet as a primary classroom for adult learners. Adult learners are people of all ages who are suitable for college education. The researchers did not mention the growing number of the virtual universities in the United States and other countries around the globe. The intention of the researchers emphasizes the negative aspects of the Internet. The researchers unintentionally reported that "The more time people spend using the Internet – the more they turn their back on the traditional media" Perhaps, they will turn their back on the traditional universities!

How many students in America enrolled in the virtual universities? What are the percentage of men and women who enrolled in the virtual universities? What are the success stories measured in incomes and status in the society? What are the incomes of the virtual university graduates in comparison to the traditional university graduates? The Internet Society is the society where the Internet students study and socialize; therefore, how the Internet students are able to function and balance their family or the military duties with the educational superiority provided by the virtual university?

The Internet Society is a sub-society in the recent years but it is the parent society of the future. What Nie and Erbring did not say is the overwhelming Internet Technology and the role of the Internet which is affecting the current society. Also the researchers of this study did not mention the Internet as a society in itself. The Internet brings people from all over the world together. The Internet provides intensive culture changes to the distant villages and communities. This study is suspicious of the new evolution and the creation of the new society's structure.

Why did Nie and Erbring ignore the fact that virtual universities provide essential services for people of all ages? The adult learners are now the majority of the virtual universities' students. The lack of data gathered about the Internet universities, in this study; denotes an intentional trend to ignore the unbeatable competitors, the virtual universities, to the shaking traditional system.

The study should include the educational evolution on the internet and how this evolution affects the speed of learning? How students who are working toward their education accomplish complicated information in a relatively short time? What is the effect of speed learning on the mind of the recipient? What is the effect of the asynchronous system on the behavior of the individual? What are the health consequences of the Internet user who is exposed to the radiation generated by the computer? What are the effects of typing constantly on the Internet user's speech level? Will the Internet user need to attend speech therapy to compensate the hours spent in the front of the computer? Will the oral conversation become the sign of the past?

What should be known about this study and it would really evaluate it effectively besides what it has been said until now are several issues. First, the comparison between the past and the future statistically should be translated in graphs. How people spend their times, for example, in 1960, 1980, and 2002. What the number of hours a student spends studying during these three periods? How many hours people used to socialize? What was the reason for the isolation in the past and now or during these three periods?

Second, the comparison between alternatives should be addressed. What are people doing if they are not on the internet? What is the reason(s) of the decline of the number of viewers who watch television or listen to radio? Is the Internet the reason for the decline or the VCR and the DVD? Third, what are the challenges and the opportunities which the users of the Internet facing? For example, what are the limitations associated with the Internet? What are the useful features associated with the Internet?

In this research which is conducted by Nie and Erbring probably the constructs were: The changes in the social behavior, isolation, economic changes, the technology of the Internet and society, the average American and the influence of the Internet especially and the technology in general, the effect of the information availability and people, and the entertainment and the consumers. Looking at the changes in the social behavior as a construct the operational definition would be what causes the behavior to change? Is the behavior of people related to the Internet? Who are the groups which are influenced by the change in technology? The variable would be gender, age, ethnics, and education. Also isolation is a construct and the operational definition will be who the groups who are affected are? What are the reasons of the isolation, is it the Internet or the fear of the criminals? Why these groups prefer to work from home; is it safer to work from home or to help raise a family? The variables are gender, races, ages, the number of the Internet activities and the hours spent on the Internet.

This case probably would be more effective if the researchers add constructs; such as, students prefer to obtain their degrees via the Internet. The Internet creates opportunities for working adults. The Internet increases the knowledge of the users. The Internet changes the methods of teaching. The Internet creates new jobs and the methods of work. The variables probably will be the number of students, their age, the type of study, the family size, and the number of students in class. Secondly, the variables for the opportunities the Internet creates for working adults are the number of job available, the hours required, and the average income. Thirdly, the Internet increases the knowledge of the users and the variables would be the number of hours spent researching, the dollar amount the user receives from updating her/his information, and the number of activities.

The researchers cannot include every construct that comes to mind. The researcher is limited by the time and the data needed to complete a research. No doubt the sponsors of a research have an agenda and they will dictate the outline for the researchers and the scope of the research. McKinsey & Co., for example, is management consulting firm and its consultation is in the area of organization technology. The increase and growing the businesses on the Internet encourages many companies to study the market to see the strength and the weakness of the Internet industry. Choosing Nie and Erbring is no accident. They both have one thing in common which is their education and experience in the quantitative methods which make the research reliable in a huge extent.

The lesson taken from this case is that the knowledge is powerful. The investigators, Nie and Erbring, did a good job collecting data to be used in the research. The survey was conducted on the Internet and the result was precise and accurate. It would be very useful for me to follow this model of thinking because the report was very informative and enjoyable.

References

Nie, N. H. & Erbring, L (2000). *Internet and Society: A Preliminary Report.* Retrieved April 3, 2003, from Website: http://graduate. tourou.edu/bus601m3/modules/module02/case.htm

About the Author

I hope you enjoyed or you will enjoy this Leadership Review Handbook!! Besides teaching in higher education for more than 8 years, I also worked as an accountant and manager/owner in my practice for over 20 years. Helping small businesses achieve their objectives professionally, dealing with their struggles to survive, and interacting with the successes and failures they encounter are valuable life experiences I treasure because they add meaning to my work and give me the sense of accomplishment.

My philosophy is that Distance Learning helps adult learners to overcome the obstacles, which they might have, that inhibit them from pursuing their education through the educational systems of the past. Recently, students of all ages are able to pursue up-to-the-minute online courses. Online courses are dynamical because they facilitate a combination of knowledge, which is exchanged in the group setting, and the use of technologies which are the tools of communication in our time and in years to come.

I am interested in writing about different subjects, watching cable channels for entertainments and world affairs, and reading the newspapers on the Internet. And during the years, I wrote poetry, short stories, minute plays, thoughts in religion and philosophy, interpretations on accounting theories and methodologies, critical reviews in business management, and I also wrote leadership reviews. I have published six books plus my dissertation in the United States and three other books have been published and distributed overseas.

EDUCATION

- **D.B.A. Financial Management,** Northcentral University, Prescott Valley, AZ

- **M.B.A. Managerial Leadership,** City University of Seattle, Bellevue, WA

- **B.S. Accounting,** Excelsior College , Albany, NY

PROFESSIONAL CERTIFICATION

- **S.C.P.M. Stanford Certified Project Manager,** Stanford University, Stanford, CA

- **Certificate in Critical Thinking Teaching Methods,** The University of Phoenix, Phoenix, AZ

Other Publications by the Author

Business Management Handbook. (AuthorHouse).

Financial Accounting Handbook. (AuthorHouse).

Analyzing the Fair Market Value of Assets and the Stakeholders' Investment Decisions. (ProQuest).

The Triune God: Philosophical Concepts and Facts. (AuthorHouse).

At the Intersections of Dundalk Avenue: A collection of Short Stories and Minute Plays. (AuthorHouse).

1ˢᵗ Sparklet of Glancing Hope: A Collection of Poetry. (AuthorHouse).

When the Sun Sets: A Collection of Poetry. (Boustany's).

A Portrait from the Past: A Collection of Poetry. (Boustany's).

Salwa: A Collection of Poetry. (Boustany's).

About the Book

This book is collected works of critical reviews in leadership which is taught in the undergraduate and the graduate levels. Throughout the book I analyzed the basic and the related concepts of leaderships. Although, I followed closely the APA formatting, but I occasionally was not restricted by its rules.

Breinigsville, PA USA
30 April 2010
237101BV00001B/45/P